The Skiers' Guide to
The Biggest Skiing in America®

By Dr. Jeff Strickler

Big Sky Resort
www.bigskyresort.com
406-995-5000

Moonlight Basin
www.moonlightbasin.com
406-995-7600

Lone Mountain Ranch
www.lmranch.com
406-995-4644

Big Sky, Montana

Printed in the United States of America

ISBN Number pending **978-0-615-43712-5**

Library of Congress Number pending

INTRODUCTION:

The Biggest Skiing in America! Uncrowded, with over 400 inches of snow a season! 5512 acres of alpine skiing on 4350 vertical feet, and with 27 lifts serving over 250 runs! The #1 rated Nordic ski center in North America with 90 km of groomed trails, and Yellowstone Park at our back door! This a truly an exceptional place.

We first skied Big Sky in 1975 when there were only four lifts and eighteen runs. Lone Mountain Ranch was still the primitive B bar K and Moonlight Basin was decades away. The subsequent 35 years saw the continued expansion of the skiing terrain. That and the growth of a permanent and friendly community lured us here to enjoy it full time in 2005. During one of our bluebird days of skiing this past Spring, my good friend Darius Larsen, pastor of the All Saints Congregation here in Big Sky, said, "You know something, Jeff. You should write a book about the mountain and the names of the runs on it." Resistant as I have been to the exhortations of preachers, it seemed to be a good idea, and this book was born.

Added to this was the need to capture some of the history of the area. Chet Huntley died in 1974 before his dream of a Montana ski resort was fully realized. Bob and Vivian Schaap retired and sold the Lone Mountain Ranch in 2007, and now Lee Poole and his partners in Moonlight Basin are moving on. It was time to document the creation of this world class ski area.

Every major ski resort, especially one this big, could use a guide to help the uninitiated. Even those who ski the mountain regularly have difficulty skiing all 250+ runs in a year, let alone in a week-long vacation. Although other "skier's guides" have been written, most are reviews or general overviews of broad areas such as Tahoe, Colorado, or Utah; or are short, magazine-sized articles or websites with superficial recommendations of the area. We created here the first comprehensive guide to a ski area that describes each of the runs on the mountain, both listed on the official trail maps, and those places known and named only by the locals and the ski patrol. It also presents all the groomed cross country trails and adds suggestions for some of the ungroomed backcountry adventures in Yellowstone.

No guide would be complete without a section suggesting where to ski what. Included are recommended days on all of the various types of runs: from greens to blues, trees to bumps, the steeps to the extremes, and some thoughts on our special powder days. Although these are just suggestions, they represent a compilation of the advice of people who ski this mountain regularly: locals, resort staff, ski patrol, and ski instructors. As such, they should lead you to some heavenly skiing, while avoiding the gnarly and ordinary. Remember that recommendations will vary with the weather and conditions, but on a mountain that has so many faces, different elevations, and varied terrain; good lines are always available somewhere.

Finally, in addition to the descriptive section, writing this book has satisfied my penchant for names and their derivation. Francis Bacon (1561-1626) had written that, "Name, though it seem but a superficial and outward matter, yet it carryieth much impression and enchantment". And Wallace Stegner, the great western author, said in his introduction to George R. Stewart's seminal work, *Names on the Land*, "that nothing is comprehended, much less possessed until it has been given a name". My earlier book, *Big Sky Names, An Amble Through Western History and Ecology on the Roads, Streams and Developments of Big Sky, Montana* dealt with the unique names in Big Sky, and how, more than just a description of location, they give us ownership and a sense of place in these mountains. So it is with the ski runs as well. Some of our trail names are of historical interest like Natawista, Crazy Horse, and Ulery's Trace. Others are just fun like the Turkey Traverse, 3 Moons, Beaver Slide, and Broken Promise. Of course there are those that commemorate some of the originals of these resorts; among others, Schaap's Schuss, Huntley Hollow, Mr K, and Cupajo. How much more fun to have successfully mastered Calamity Jane or spent a day hiking up Siberia than to have skied "that run to the right of the lift with the big headwall" or have done "that long uphill thingy". With ownership comes enjoyment and sharing 35 years of that pleasure with you.

The concept of a comprehensive guide has received the enthusiastic support of the three resorts on Lone Mountain that now make up "The Biggest Skiing in America". Hopefully, it will receive the same from readers, visitors and locals alike. So prepare to be amused by the derivations of the names, appreciate getting a little better acquainted with the area, and truly enjoy skiing or riding The Biggest Skiing in America.

-- Dr Jeff Strickler, October 2010

TABLE OF CONTENTS:

RESOURCES

The daily snow report is available online from any of the resort or Chamber websites. It is also available from the Big Sky Snow Phone at 406-995-5900 or Moonlight's Snow Phone at 406-993-6666.

Lone Mountain Ranch grooming and conditions can he found by calling the outdoor shop at 406-995-4734.

For those looking for more information, I would recommend the websites of the three resorts. There you will find snow reports, trail maps, and rates; as well as information about lodging, dining, shopping, tours, activities, snowsports schools, and the like.

www.bigskyresort.com
www.lmranch.com
www.moonlightbasin.com
www.biggestskiinginamerica.com

In addition the Big Sky Chamber of Commerce website is full of information about activities, events, shopping and services available in the community.

www.bigskychamber.com

A driving map of Big Sky and links to the resorts is on the State of Montana tourism website at:

www.visitmt.com (search Big Sky)

SUGGESTED DAYS ON THE SLOPES

GREEN DAYS:

If you are a novice skier, but have passed beyond the Magic Carpet/ Conveyor stage, our ski areas have a wealth of options for your enjoyment.

Moonlight Basin's Derringer Lift at 422' by the Madison Lodge, or the Pony Express at 539' over near Moonlight Lodge serve exclusively learning areas. Spend your Derringer time on the bottom end of Wagon Train or Cinnabar. Take Stage Fright under the lift, or any of the variations - Springville, Glacier Way, Cupajo, Buckaroo, Giddy-Up and Yaak. If you are over at the Pony Express, the run of that name as well as Bootlegger and Gambler through the residential area will take you back to the base of the Pony Express. Or you can zip back over to the Madison Lodge via Natawista, Cinnabar, or the variations along Hideaway, Smithy, Drover or Alpine Meadows. These can fill a couple days of fun. But when you are ready for something longer take the Six Shooter lift. This will take you up 1850' on Montana's longest lift, and Lazy Jack from the top to Cinnabar is green all the way.

The 622' Explorer lift at **Big Sky** serves only green runs and a whole day can be had cruising Lower Mr K, Lone Wolf and White Wing. All are gentle, easy runs. Lone Wolf is wide and flat. White Wing, with its broad valley allows for big sweeping turns up the sides, and Lower Mr K gets you ready for its big brother.

When you are ready for the longer greens, I recommend starting with Mr K. This three mile long run keeps a steady pitch and seems to go on forever. It's not crowded, and being so long means that you have fewer trips getting on and off the lift. The only limitation is your energy and need for après ski libations.

There are a number of other good long green runs at Big Sky. Off the 1647' Swiftcurrent chair Lower Morning Star and Mr K are good for several laps. For more variation, another day should be spent on the Southern Comfort side of Andesite. Take the Ramcharger lift from the base and go straight ahead when you get off. The *Yellow Brick Road* is a track to your right about 100 yards down Ponderosa that leads over to Eldorado, Sacajawea, and Deep South - giving lots of choices of lovely greens. Eldorado is especially wide and mellow, and all are served by the 1250' Southern Comfort high speed quad lift. When your legs are tired, the return to the base down the Ramcharger side via Pacifier is easy and avoids all of the steep blues.

BLUE DAYS FOR CRUISING:

As a general rule, it can be said that the blue cruisers at **Moonlight Basin** tend to be more of the green square, and are easier than those at Big Sky. Meriwether from the Six Shooter, and the lovely trio from the Lone Tree lift - Horseshoe, Trembler and Lookout Ridge are all beautifully groomed for long easy cruising.

The Iron Horse lift is used by both resorts and Blue Moon and Powder River are a bit more challenging, but still nice blue cruisers. They have the added advantage of being close to Moonlight Lodge for lunch or refreshments at the bar.

Big Sky's blue cruisers are legendary, and there are plenty to pick and choose from, Ponderosa and Safari are the easiest and the ones to start with. Next, go on to Elk Park Ridge, the quintessential blue cruiser. Considered by many to be the best cruiser run in the country, its sustained pitch goes all the way to the bottom on the Thunderwolf side. Its partner, Bighorn, is wide with big sweeping turns and varied pitches. Both can be reached from any of the Andesite lifts, and are good for a couple of laps. After these delights, switch to the Ramcharger side of Andesite and ski the blues from north to south, taking in Silver Knife, Tippy's Tumble, Ambush, and Hangman's ending up back at the base area. To continue your great blue cruiser day go up the Swiftcurrent lift to do Calamity Jane and Lobo, both very interesting runs with great variation. Skier Services will have the grooming report, but all of these are generally in fine condition. If you still have legs, you can reprise any or all of your favorites.

BLUE DAYS FOR BUMPS:

Mountain skiing and moguls go together; something everyone should work to master. Rather than letting them beat up on you, the Snow Sports instructors at both resorts are there to help you learn the bump technique.

Moonlight Basin's best bumps tend to be found on the more difficult black diamonds. However the blue Riffle off Powder River provides a short mogul run that has the advantage of an escape half way down on the cat track to Moonlight Lodge. There are also blue bumps along Stillwater Traverse and on Jackrabbit along Horseshoe Bowl.

The blue mogul runs at **Big Sky** are made for learning. Marmot Meadows off Mr K is the starter. It is short, and not too steep. However, the best run for learning moguls is Africa. You can cruise into the smaller ones from Safari, leaving an escape back to this groomer. As you move more to skier's left on Africa the moguls get bigger, and the snow tends to be deeper. At the bottom, the bumps get quite big, but this is a short section, and it is not a serious steep. Over on Thunderwolf, Elk Park Meadows with its mellow pitch and mild moguls can be sweet in fresh snow, and the left, ungroomed side of Bighorn is a great exercise. Madison Avenue is sometimes groomed, and allows you to work up to the bigger bumps on lower Mad Wolf, or stay in the valley. Riffle, mentioned above, and Lobo Meadows also have manageable sized moguls and Crazy Horse can be quite "interesting". Work out on Africa, but try them all so that you will be ready to move on to the big boys on the black diamonds.

2

BLACK DAYS -- GLADE SKIING:

Both areas have superb "tree runs". Big Sky's tend to be steeper and tighter, with a tendency to more debris underfoot. Moonlight's are generally longer, going over a series of drops. In either case, don't ski the glades alone, and helmets are recommended. You will need to be able to ski the moguls that form on the lines dictated by the trees, and to be able to turn and brake on command. Everyone has favorite runs, but for a day in the trees at each resort, here is a suggestion:

For **Moonlight Basin**, ski the glades off Lookout Ridge from the Lone Tree lift: Start with the easiest which is Whiskey. Progress on to Single Jack, Double Jack, Marshall, and Trapline. Each is a bit longer and more difficult than the former. Finish with a drop down Broken Heart or the alternate, Lone Tree South, to the Big Tree Cutoff to the bottom and a well deserved rest.

A tour of the Andesite trees at **Big Sky** makes a great day. Start off on the Ramcharger lift and take Safari to Congo. This is the easiest, shortest, and most open of all the Big Sky glades. Its consistent pitch makes it everyone's favorite. Continue on around the mountain doing Wounded Knee between Hangman's and Ambush next. Follow this with Ambush Glades, Blackfoot, and the Blue Room, all of which return to the base area and Ramcharger. Take Colter's Hell next. At the road you can decide whether to turn left for an easy return to Rancharger or right to the Elevator Shaft on War Dance and the Thunderwolf lift. The last two glades are on the Thunderwolf side and are entered from gates on the left side of the top of Bighorn. Both are long, steep and tight, but the Bear Lair is the easier and has several interesting lines. The Snake Pit is a true double black diamond, one of the more difficult on the mountain. If you have had difficulty in the Bear Lair, do not try this. Rather, go back and reprise your favorite on the front side before your beer.

BLACK DAYS -- BLACK DIAMONDS AND BUMPS:

The steeps are what has made these two resorts famous. Please be careful, if you try these runs. Make sure of your skill level by gradually increasing the difficulty, and take a lesson from the Snow Sports schools if you are unsure. Wear a helmet at all times, and, because this is avalanche country, never ski alone, and always carry your transceiver, shovel and probe.

Big Sky Day 1, Andesite:

Before the Challenger lift was built, Mad Wolf was the signature black diamond. With its cornice and long series of moguls, it is still a good workout. It is big and wide so there are many lines and worth a couple of laps. Next, try Crazy Raven into Broken Arrow and the Rock Pocket. From the bottom of Thunderwolf, take the road down to the bottom of the Lone Moose lift. Here the uncrowded runs of Bobcat, Grizzly Bear, and Lone Moose can entertain you. Return via the South Glade to Bighorn, then up Thunderwolf to take a favorite run on the Ramcharger side to the base.

Big Sky Day 2, Challenger:

   Take the Swiftcurrent lift from the base area and follow the Jay Walk and BRT Traverse or Black and Blue to the Challenger. With its different faces, conditions will vary from run to run, and you can pick the best. All of the runs from this lift are "expert only" Moonlight is the "easier way down" but is a true black diamond. When BRT Traverse comes out of the woods, you can look up at the Challenger runs. If this makes you uncomfortable, the Fast Lane is just below BRT Traverse on Challenger and a right turn here will return to the base and more civilized skiing. If you end up at the Challenger lift by mistake and don't want to go up, the Bozeman trail behind the lift is a slow but safe return.

   You can spend all day exploring the black diamond challengers from the top of the lift. Start with Moonlight, wide open with big, rhythmic moguls. Follow this with Midnight, and next the Country Club to the Highway. For your next lap take the Highway again, but stay up on the ridge under the lift to the double black 17 Green. Like the double black? Go back up and take Moonlight again, but cut right to BRT North; or you can do Country Club to the Zucchini Patch instead. Both routes are great. You still haven't done Outer Limits, far left of Moonlight, where you can exit left onto the "cliff area" (it's short) or straight into Midnight Trees. (they're tight) Both lead to a return along the Fast Lane. Still have legs? Reprise your favorite (there are so many good lines) or try BRT Main. Pant, pant!

Big Sky Day 3, Up High:

   The Bowl at the top of the Lone Peak Triple chair was the only black diamond when Big Sky opened in 1974. It is still a great run, wide open and generally mogully, it can be flat as a billiard table after wind and snow. Wide as it is, there are several lines worth your time, from the *Slot* through the mid-Bowl to the Low Bench and *Mary's Bush*. Keep going around on the Turkey Traverse for runs down the South Wall and Black Rock.

   Fun as the Bowl area is, you need to go to the top, and a ride up the Tram is worth the price of admission itself. Liberty Bowl is the black diamond off the top and the "easiest route" down. If it is too intimidating, take the Tram back down. Lots of people do this. When you get to the trees at the bottom of the bowl section of Liberty, you can turn right for some fun in the Dakota Territory, or go straight on Screaming Left to the Shedhorn. Here the blacks of Yellow Mule, Larkspur and Dude Park will entertain you. You can cruise all the way back off the Duck Walk and the Jay Walk, but you should finish with another black. When you get to the top of the Swiftcurrent lift, take Lobo Meadows and go straight into the Stump Farm before you collapse at the Mall.

Moonlight Basin is mostly famous for its greens, its trees and its double black steeps. However, there are several black diamond bump runs that will give a good workout and pleasure to boot.

Your Moonlight Black Day:

Elkhorn is the easiest black diamond on the mountain. Steep only for the first couple hundred yards, it mellows into a blue cruiser. It should be your introduction. If it intimidates you, take a lesson and avoid the steeper black diamonds until you are more skilled.

From the Iron Horse lift, Bad Dog, Snake Bite, and Iron Maiden will test your mogul skills. Then go over to the Lone Tree lift. On any day, but particularly good snow days, Lone Tree North and South, Obsidian, and Broken Heart can be a special experience.

DOUBLE BLACK DAYS:

Big Sky

The signature extreme run at Big Sky is the Big Couloir. This requires a sign out with the ski patrol at the top of the Tram, a partner, transceiver, probe, and shovel. Helmets are strongly recommended. If you do not have an experienced partner, it is best done by hiring a guide from the Ski School in the Snowcrest building at the base of the Swiftcurrent lift.

Outside of "The Big" there are a host of steep and interesting double black diamond runs on this mountain, most of which revolve off the Tram. Remember that you will be skiing above 11,000 feet where the lower oxygen will sap your strength and you will need to keep hydrated. Be prepared for wind and cold, and always wear your helmet and carry your transceiver, probe, and shovel.

As a suggested day, it is recommended that you start with a warm-up on the South Wall of the Bowl. If this is intimidating, then stay off the double blacks on the top and do Liberty Bowl. If you find the South Wall fun, head up the Tram for some "laps". Take the Yeti Traverse which starts left a little way down Liberty and leads to Lenin and Marx. Do these in either order as both end up nearly together on the Duck Walk for a return to the Triple chair and the Tram.

Next, take a variation off of Lenin - do the right shoulder to one of the Dictator Chutes, Castro's, or The Wave. All are fun and steep. The farther right you go, the harder it is to get back to the Duck Walk and you will need to go down Sunlight to the Shedhorn lift for your return lap.

Follow this with a variation off Marx. Staying high on skier's left will take you to the powder lines on Tohelluride, or past the little sign up the ridge to the Dirtbag Wall. Both of these return via the Duck Walk. The most popular variation from Marx is to take the Gullies. The traverse is about a quarter the way down Marx on the left, and leads over the ridge to the Gullies which descend into the Bowl. The recommended one is First Gully, farthest left, as it is the widest. If the snow is low and it is rocky through the rock band, halfway down, swing left to Cron's. This short traverse over the ridge leads to a wall used for Powder 8s competition and on to Cue Ball and the Tram.

Moonlight Basin:

The signature extreme run here is the North Summit Snowfield. This starts from the top of the Tram, and so will require a Biggest Skiing in America pass, or both a Big Sky and Moonlight Basin pass to ride up. You will need to sign out with the ski patrol at the Moonlight hut on top, and go in a scheduled group with a maximum of 4 people. Helmets are strongly recommended, and transceiver, probe, and shovel are required. This is very steep, extreme skiing, so go with a knowledgeable partner, or hire a guide at the SnowSports school. RIPS is a bit easier than Great Falls off the Snowfield, but both lead into the beautiful open powder field on Deepwater Bowl.

Moonlight Basin is also famous for the double black diamonds off The Headwaters. The runs near the Headwaters lift are steep, fun, and have an easy return to the lift for laps. One can get to this area with a little hike to the lift from the top of the Six Shooter, or with a Biggest Skiing in America or Big Sky pass, from the top of the Challenger lift. Start with the chute closest to the lift, also called Headwaters. On successive laps do Alder Gulch, Cold Spring, and Firehole; then repeat your favorites as your spirit demands and your legs allow. The named runs to the left of Firehole are not recommended.

POWDER DAYS:

With 400+ inches of snow a season and the dry, cold Montana climate, this mountain gets lots of true powder. This is perhaps the most enjoyable of skiing experiences, and we get it often. Although the technique is essentially the same as skiing groomers, it can be intimidating to those who are not used to it. Our SnowSports schools at both Moonlight Basin and Big Sky would love to help you master the powder.

For the uninitiated, a 3" to 6" snowfall on our blue groomers like Tippy's, Silverknife, Lookout Ridge, or Calamity Jane are great starters. The consistent groomed base gives the confidence to let your skis float while maintaining speed and practicing patient turns. Even the greens like Natawista, Sacajawea, and Deep South can have fun powder if not too deep and slow.

But for Powder Hounds, the best lines are away from the groomed runs. First tracks are often best on Elk Park Meadows. Not too steep, and with a huge wide slope to choose from, this is usually good for several laps before it is too cut up for "Freshies". The next site is up to the Bowl. Because the new snow causes avalanche danger, the Bowl opening is often delayed on snow days until 10:00 or 11:00 for control efforts. Be in line at the Triple when the charges stop going off to be one of the first up the lift. A whole series of lines from *the Slot* on the left to *Mary's Bush* on the right, or farther over the Turkey Traverse to Black Rock and the South Wall give lots of lines for fresh tracks.

The Shedhorn or "Shredhorn" is another great area for powder. Dude Park with its widely spaced trees and big rollers is particularly sweet; as is the open field on the right of Larkspur. Over on Challenger BRT North and 17 Green are favorites.

For bumps in the powder, Moonlight's Lone Tree runs and Big Sky's Africa and Mad Wolf near the trees to skier's right are the best.

Although whiteout visibility can be a problem if it is snowing up high, the powder can be particularly good on the runs off the Tram. Deep snow will slow you down and allow you to float like a cloud down the double blacks. With the prevailing wind from the west. Marx tends to pick up extra deep snow blown over from Liberty.

And the trees! Moonlight Basin's glade runs are famous in themselves, but after a good snowfall, they are spectacular. The above suggested series of Whiskey, Single and Double Jack, Marshall to Trapline is as good as it gets, but explore them all. Over at Big Sky, the relatively open Congo is good if hit early, and the best snow collects in the Blue Room and Colter's Hell.

Late in the day the best powder is wherever you can find it. The regular runs are usually skied off, so try some of the out of the way places. Snoop for stashes in the trees, head for the Dakota Territory, or try Rice Bowl, Chuck's Run or Grizzly Meadows. Wherever it is, they are your tracks and your pleasure.

These are just some suggested days for fun on the slopes. This is "The Biggest Skiing in America", and many more challenges, both on the trail maps and unlisted, abound. The author tries to ski a run or line each day that he hasn't skied before that season. With 258 named runs on the maps, and another 52 in this book that are not on the map, it is not a difficult task. So go out and enjoy where your skill and spirit take you. Schi Heil!!!

SUGGESTIONS FROM THE LOCAL KIDS:

Skiing and riding are not just for the big people. Kids have more fun at whatever they do, and they do it with no fear and greater abandon. Anyone who has watched the small people schuss and wiggle down the slopes can only wish that they had been able to start at that age.

To this end, I decided to ask the local kids about their favorite runs, and if there were any special places that they knew about that the adults didn't. I had the good fortune to be invited to Ophir School to interview the 4th graders in Mr. Harder's class and the 6th graders from Mr. Neal's. They lit into the interview with enthusiasm and I would especially like to thank Justin, Kuka, Harrison, Katie, Howie, Carter. Brett, Michelle, Anna, Dakota, and all the others who aren't named. If you appreciate the fact that these kids live in Big Sky and ski regularly with their parents on weekends and with the school program during the week; you will know that they are very skilled at a very young age. Some of these 10-12 year olds have skied the North Summit Snowfield and the Big Couloir. Take their recommendations with this in mind.

Fun Runs: The Natural Half Pipe
Cruisers: Hangman's (Its good for racing)
Moguls: Elkhorn
     Congo
Trees: Blue Room
     trees off the bottom of the Natural Half Pipe
      (don't turn onto Lower Morning Star)
     White Fang
Steeps: The Headwaters - (especially Firehole)
     Liberty Bowl
Powder Stashes: Beacon Park
Jumps: on Fast Lane coming off the Six Shooter
Special Kids trails (They named them!):
     Banana Land
      "Great trees" to skier's left in Congo
     Awesome Trail - also known as Alaska Trail
      The set of trees at the bottom of Swifty Terrain Park
     Nameless Trail
      A series of jumps and trails weaving through the trees off of Mr K
     Tunnel Trees
      Along Mr K on the right and a bit further in the woods

A note of caution: The kids tree runs have branches at grade schooler's height. The 6' 5" author suffered some serious and painful humiliation following his 9 year old granddaughter in here.

Big Sky Resort Mountain Village   *Glenniss Indreland*

BIG SKY RESORT

Big Sky Resort was the vision of famous NBC news anchor Chet Huntley who was born just a few miles north west of here in Cardwell, MT. With a consortium of Chrysler Realty, Northwest Airlines, Burlington Northern Railways, and others, the dream took shape, and the ski area opened for the 1973-74 season. At that time there were only four lifts, "Andesite" where Ramcharger is now, a gondola, now replaced by the Swiftcurrent high speed quad, the Explorer, and the Triple Chair to the Bowl. There were only 18 runs and the Huntley Lodge on the mountain did not open until the following season. The Spur Road, Lone Mountain Trail, was unpaved and a black diamond adventure in itself. In 1976 the resort was purchased by Boyne Resorts and steady improvements ensued. Over the next 35 years the expansion has found 21 lifts and 156 named runs, the addition of numerous condos, two world class hotels, and a growing full time community in the Meadow Village. The Tram to the black diamond terrain at the top of the mountain, along with the association with Moonlight Basin and Lone Mountain Ranch as "The Biggest Skiing in America" has further enriched the skiing. But what really distinguishes this mountain is all the different exposures and terrain. Runs are found from true South facing in the Dakota Territory, around to the East off Swiftcurrent and North to Northwest at Moonlight Basin. There are multiple faces off Challenger; three directions off Andesite; the low, sheltered valley for the Lone Moose runs; and glades galore. That means that you can always find a good turn, excellent snow or a run out of the wind. Then with an average of 400 inches - that's 33 feet! - of dry powder a season, you will find in Big Sky one of the world's great ski experiences.

The following alphabetical list represents all of the current runs available on the mountain. Those that are not on the official trail map are listed in italics and avalanche routes are signified as a little **a**. Green dots ● are easiest, blue squares ■ are intermediate runs, and black diamonds ♦ are expert, with double black diamonds ♦♦ the extreme terrain. Please be aware that all these classes are relative, and this is big mountain skiing. Thus, some of our blues may be considered blacks elsewhere, and the expert black diamonds may be significantly more difficult than you are used to. Remember, too, that regular grooming and a wide expanse may lower a category in spite of the pitch, whereas big moguls, trees and other hazards may step it up. All references to direction are to the skier's right and left unless otherwise noted.

9

That said, have a read, pick your lines, and have a great day on the slopes.

The daily snow report is on the Snow Phone at 406-995-5900 or online. Those interested in more information should visit www.bigskyresort.com.

BIG SKY TRAILS CHECKLIST
These represent all of the trails listed on the official Big Sky trail map, as well as the unofficial named trails in *italics*. Trail maps are available at the ticket window and from Skier Services, and are on the mountain stats and trail map section of the Big Sky website.

GREEN:
- ☐ Bear Back
- ☐ Bozeman Trail
- ☐ Chet's Knob
- ☐ Deep South
- ☐ Eldorado
- ☐ Freemont's Forest
- ☐ *Feral*
- ☐ Jay Walk
- ☐ *Guilford's Ladder*
- ☐ Little Calf
- ☐ Little Dogie
- ☐ Little Ewe
- ☐ Little Thunder
- ☐ Lone Moose Access
- ☐ Lone Wolf
- ☐ Lower Morning Star
- ☐ *Magnum Couloir*
- ☐ Mr K
- ☐ Natural Half Pipe
- ☐ *Nameless Trail*
- ☐ Pacifier
- ☐ Sacajawea
- ☐ Saddle Ridge Access
- ☐ Safari
- ☐ *Tunnel Trees*
- ☐ Twin Tunnels Access
- ☐ Wapiti
- ☐ White Fang
- ☐ White Wing
- ☐ *Yellow Brick Road*

REAL ESTATE ACCESS:
- ☐ Cascade
- ☐ Middle Rider
- ☐ Rising Bull
- ☐ Rosebud
- ☐ White Otter

BLUE CRUISERS:
- ☐ Ambush
- ☐ Bighorn
- ☐ Black and Blue
- ☐ Blue Moon
- ☐ BRT Road
- ☐ Calamity Jane
- ☐ Cow Flats
- ☐ Crazy Horse
- ☐ Duck Walk
- ☐ Elk Park Ridge
- ☐ Fast Lane
- ☐ Hangman's
- ☐ Hippy Highway
- ☐ Huntley Hollow
- ☐ Lobo
- ☐ Middle Road
- ☐ Ponderosa
- ☐ Powder River
- ☐ Silver Knife
- ☐ Sunlight
- ☐ *Three Forks*
- ☐ Tippy's Tumble
- ☐ Upper Morning Star

BLUE BUMPS:
- ☐ *Ambush South*
- ☐ Africa
- ☐ Chuck's Run
- ☐ Lobo Meadows
- ☐ Madison Avenue
- ☐ Marmot Meadows
- ☐ Old Tippy's
- ☐ Riffle
- ☐ Swifty Lift Line

BLUE GLADES:
- ☐ Ambush Meadows
- ☐ *Awesome Trail*
-    *Alaska Trail*
- ☐ Elk Park Meadows
- ☐ South Glades

BLACK GLADES:
- ☐ Ambush Glades
- ☐ Aspen Meadows
- ☐ *Banana Land*
- ☐ Bavarian Forest
- ☐ Bear Lair
- ☐ Blackfoot
- ☐ Blue Room
- ☐ Cardio Trio
- ☐ *Challenger Trees*
- ☐ Colter's Hell
- ☐ Congo
- ☐ Dakota Gully
- ☐ Dead Top
- ☐ Dude Park
- ☐ Erica's Glade
- ☐ *Forested Knoll*
- ☐ *Gondola Shaft*
- ☐ Great White
- ☐ *Keyhole*
- ☐ Larkspur
- ☐ Low Dog
- ☐ Magic Meadows
- ☐ Mine Shaft
- ☐ *Mora's*
- ☐ Mule Skinner
- ☐ Packsaddle Glades
- ☐ Paradise
- ☐ *Ray's Ridge*

- ☐ Rice Bowl
- ☐ St Alphonse Trees
- ☐ Tango Trees
- ☐ Todd's Hole
- ☐ *Tower 10*
- ☐ *Twilight*
- ☐ War Dance
- ☐ Wounded Knee
- ☐ *Yogi's Hat*
- ☐ Zucchini Patch

BLACK BUMPS:
- ☐ 3 Moons
- ☐ Arch Rock
- ☐ *Arm Chair*
- ☐ Bad Dog
- ☐ *Ball Buster*
- ☐ Black Rock Gully
- ☐ *Bob's Corner*
- ☐ Bobcat
- ☐ Bone Crusher
- ☐ *Booger Nugget Nose*
- ☐ The Bowl
- ☐ Broken Arrow
- ☐ Buffalo Jump
- ☐ *Challenger Lift Line*
- ☐ *Chippewa Notch*
- ☐ *The Clevage*
- ☐ Country Club
- ☐ Crazy Raven
- ☐ Dakota Territory
- ☐ Dead Top
- ☐ *Everett's Anger*
- ☐ Grizzly Bear
- ☐ Gullies Traverse
- ☐ Gun Mount
- ☐ High Clearing
- ☐ Highway
- ☐ Iron Maiden
- ☐ Jock Strap
- ☐ Liberty Bowl
- ☐ Lone Moose
- ☐ Low Bench
- ☐ Low Clearing
- ☐ Mad Wolf

- ☐ *Mary's Bush*
- ☐ Midnight
- ☐ Moonlight
- ☐ Never Sweat
- ☐ *Parkin's Paradise*
- ☐ Pinnacles
- ☐ *Rainbow Rock*
- ☐ Screaming Left
- ☐ *Slot*
- ☐ Snake Bite
- ☐ South Wall
- ☐ Stump Farm
- ☐ Stutzman's Rock
- ☐ Turkey Traverse
- ☐ Upper Africa
- ☐ *Wyoming Bowl*
- ☐ Yellow Mule

DOUBLE BLACKS:
- ☐ 17 Green
- ☐ A-Z Chutes
      Biff's
      Mick Jagger's Lip
      Parachute
      Rick's Danger
      Stranglehold
      Z Chute
- ☐ Bacon Rind
- ☐ Big Couloir
- ☐ Big Rock Tongue
- ☐ Bolivia
- ☐ BRT North
- ☐ Cache Trees
- ☐ Castro's
- ☐ Cron's
- ☐ *Cue Ball*
- ☐ Dictator Chutes
- ☐ Dirt Bag Wall
- ☐ *Dobe's*
- ☐ Exit Chute
- ☐ Gullies
- ☐ Hanging Valley
- ☐ Kircher's Cliffs
- ☐ Lenin
- ☐ *Little Couloir*
- ☐ Little Gullies

- ☐ *Little Mussolini*
- ☐ Little Rock Tongue
- ☐ Little Tree
- ☐ Marlboro Country
- ☐ Marx
- ☐ Onslow's
- ☐ Otter Slide
- ☐ Outer Limits
- ☐ Peru
- ☐ *Rat Hole's Revenge*
- ☐ Rock Pocket
- ☐ Rockville Bowl
- ☐ *Secret Entrance*
- ☐ *Shady Chute*
- ☐ *Short Shot*
- ☐ Snake Pit
- ☐ South Face
- ☐ *Sure Shot*
- ☐ The Wave
- ☐ Todd's Hole
- ☐ Tohelluride
- ☐ Vuarnet Cliffs
- ☐ Yeti Traverse

BIG SKY TRAIL DESCRIPTIONS

3 MOONS ♦ a

One hikes to this chute by taking the ridge above the Challenger lift, arriving just short of the A-Z Chutes. It is steep and very challenging, and even the hike will give you a thrill.

Two Moons

It was originally thought that this name was an attempt for those on the mountain to one up the Meadow Village, since the latter has a Two Moons Road. Not so! The road was named for a famous Northern Cheyenne chief who lived around 1900. This run's name has a more skierish origin. In the early days when the Challenger terrain was hiking only, three patrollers were up at the start of the run and saw some buddies on a groomer below. Naturally delighted with their good fortune, and contemptuous of their lazy colleagues, they signaled them by dropping trou and giving them...

Three Moons

17 GREEN ♦ ♦

Access to this fun but steeply challenging run comes by staying high on the Highway off the Challenger lift or by traversing across the bottom of the Country Club and past the dead trees to the lift line. It then drops steeply along the lift to the run-out of BRT and the BRT Traverse. Double black diamonds require expert skill and knowledge of self arrest technique. This is, however, perhaps the easiest of this category on the mountain, and the first one to try if you feel up to the double blacks.

Often mistakenly called the 17th Green because it can be accessed off the Country Club, it actually comes from St Patrick's Day, March 17. On that day in the late 1970s a big avalanche slid down this run.

A-Z CHUTES ♦ ♦

This series of extreme chutes are accessed by hiking up from the Challenger lift along the ridgeline, or by climbing straight up from the bottom. Extremely steep, skiers and boarders descend into the cirque west of the tram house and provide entertainment for people waiting in line.

Called A to Z because of the regular arrangement, some have been given specific names by the ski patrol. Biff's was named for Ian Schlossman, a local guitarist and singer who was frequently heard in the local bars in the early '80s. The chute called Rick's Danger was named for a local who had to be evacuated

12

from it via a rope. Mick Jagger's Lip is the only chute with a persistent cornice. (get it?) Stranglehold comes from a radio transmission from an angry patrol director threatening to come up and strangle the miscreant. Parachute is obviously for the steep that resembles jumping out of an airplane. Z Chute, because it is at the far right as you look up, at the end of the row, next to the Pinnacles.

AFRICA ■ UPPER AFRICA ♦

Like our southern continent, Africa, this is the southernmost run off the Ramcharger side of Andesite. It also originally looked like the shape of the continent of Africa from a distance. More logging has opened up the run for better skiing, and much of the African shape has disappeared.

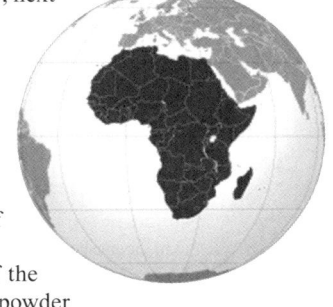

Africa, Wikipedia

Upper Africa comes directly off the top of the Southern Comfort lift and can have a couple of nice powder turns before reaching Pacifier. However, wind comes straight up the run, and the narrow, steep section before Pacifier is quickly scraped off, so this run is usually closed for lack of snow.

Africa itself is one of the better runs to practice your mogul technique. The pitch is consistent and not too steep. Safari, on the right side of Africa, is groomed, and gives an escape if the bumps beat you up. The official entry is from Pacifier, traversing across the top of Africa. The entry from Safari is easier as it avoids the steeper, and sometimes rocky bumps section. Because of the prevailing wind and the shelter of the belt of trees, the best snow is often found by taking Pacifier to the trees at the left of Africa, and following the line down skier's farthest left through the bigger bumps.

AMBUSH ■ MEADOWS ■ AND GLADES♦

Although altered for better intermediate skiing, the original run under the old Ramshorn chair was not cut in the fall line and was nicknamed "slambush". Skiers had to make a series of short turn - long turn descents to stay on the fall line. Any attempt to get rhythmic turns and you would end up "ambushed" by the trees. It is now a well groomed, open, wide run that is great for perfecting your GS turns.

Ambush Meadows ■ is a wide open, rarely groomed glade that starts off the Andesite cat track about 100 yards beyond the main Ambush entrance. Good for working on irregular, untracked conditions, the trees are spaced far enough apart to not be threatening. It was formerly the site of the big terrain park with monster jumps and rails. Infrequent use, the huge amount of work and expense to maintain, combined with the risk of the huge jumps, resulted in its removal in recent years. The only remaining feature is the bit of the halfpipe that was cut into the hill below the Ramcharger lift.

Ambush South ■ follows the Ramcharger lift line as it parallels the groomed Ambush. Narrow and bumpy, it allows showing off your bump technique to the lift riders. As close as it is to the lift, your miscues will also be recorded for posterity.

Now, we love to ski the trees, and glade runs have been opened all over

Andesite. Ambush Glades ♦ is one of the nicest. It can be entered from Ambush Meadows and keeping right until you see the sign at the wall of trees.   It can also be found by heading towards Tippy's and Silverknife and turning left onto the little road a couple hundred yards down *Three Forks*. A right turn as this road opens onto Ambush Meadows will again get to the sign on the wall of trees. Fear not! The trees quickly open up onto one of the loveliest glades at Big Sky with lots of bumps, open trees and small meadows. It returns to Ambush at the bottom end of the half pipe. Stay under the lift for the bumps, or angle out below the half pipe to the final Ambush headwall.

ANDESITE

The name of one of our mountains comes from the scientific name for this dark colored volcanic rock. Frequently found at the edge of tectonic plates, the rock is named for the Andes Mountain range of South America. Ramcharger, Thunderwolf and Southern Comfort ski lifts are on Andesite Mountain. Dr. Dave Lageson, ski patroller and professor of Geology at Montana State University, points out that the rock on Andesite Mountain is actually a closely related form called dacite porphyry. However, saying, "come on, let's go to Dacite Porphyry and cut some turns in the glades!" doesn't sound right, so we'll stick with Andesite.

ARCH ROCK ♦

This line was named for the rock that sits above this chute towards the far end of the South Wall of the Bowl.   Bouncing along the Turkey Traverse to the end is rewarded by this very steep, if short, line.

ARM CHAIR ♦

Another unofficial line that was named for a rock, this odd looking formation marks a line off the South Wall between Arch Rock and the Exit Chute. All of the descents off the South Wall are steep black diamonds that demand expert technique. They are, however, short, and a good place to practice before tackling the bigger runs off the Tram.

Below the start of this line are a pair of roller rocks that tend to get blown off, leaving *The Cleavage* between for your pleasure.

ASPEN MEADOWS ♦

Take Liberty Bowl to the trees at the bottom of the bowl, then follow the ridge along the top right of Screaming Left. Go through the gate at the end and past the sign for Erica's Glade to come out on a lovely, wide open meadow dotted with aspens. The initial trees are tight, but quick, and the Meadows often have powder when it has been skied off elsewhere. The run exits out on the Hippy Highway and on to the base of the Shedhorn lift.

Populus tremuloides, The quaking, or golden aspen, is the only deciduous tree in our high forests. One of the first plants to invade an area after a fire, the aspen usually reproduces by sending out suckers, which explains why it appears in groves. Being all the same genetic plant, these groves all leaf out or turn golden at the same time. The leaf stem of the aspen is flattened rather than round and is flexible near the leaf blade. This allows for the fluttering that gives the characteristic quaking sound, and accounts for the Native American name that translates as "woman's tongue".

AWESOME TRAIL ■
Also called the *Alaska Trail*, these trees off the end of the Swifty Lift Line terrain park gives a variation to the groomed return to the base. It is a favorite of the Ophir School kids.

BACON RIND ♦ ♦
This tight, steep glade between Packsaddle and Paradise off the Duck Walk is another run in the Shedhorn that is named for a local geographic feature.

Bacon Rind Creek is just south of Big Sky in Yellowstone Park. It flows east from the Madison Range and enters the Gallatin River near milepost 22. It is said to be named because of an old hunk of bacon found in the creek attracted bears. It makes a good short hike in the summer, and one of the best backcountry skis in the winter.

BAD DOG ♦
This short drop off to the left of Fast Lane is a good workout on moguls. While you can enter off the Fast Lane from the Iron Horse lift, it also makes a nice extension of Challenger's Moonlight run if you want to go to Iron Horse or Moonlight Lodge rather than returning to the Challenger lift. Midway down Bad Dog the Saddle Ridge access cat track cuts across, giving an escape to the Lodge. Continuing down leads to the bottom of Riffle and on to the Iron Horse lift.

Native American in sound, there is no specific reference to such an individual. Be careful that the bad dog doesn't jump up from the moguls and grab your leg.

BALL BUSTER ♦
The generally closed and roped off bottom section of Larkspur goes directly under the Shedhorn lift. Because of poor snow coverage, stumps and debris, skiers are directed away from this area and down Jock Strap or over to Yellow Mule.

This is a location name, but not a place to try, particularly because of the derivation of the name. The story is that a notorious skier and Bozeman native, Kelly Ball, had to be evacuated out of here after he ducked under the closure rope and tried to ski down it. He injured his nether regions on a stump, so his name and injury led to calling this run the Ball Buster.

BANANA LAND ♦
An area favorite of the local kids, they have named the trees to the left of Congo, "Banana Land." Slippery, monkey food, insanity... you can choose your own reason for the derivation of the name.

BAVARIAN FOREST ♦

This run, actually an area, was named in the 80s when the access came off Liberty Bowl and you skied deep trees to the Hippy Highway for a return to the Shedhorn lift. With the installation of the Dakota Lift, the forest has been thinned significantly, with many nice routes down through the trees. The Dakota lift allows for repeated enjoyment without the need to go all the way around back up the Tram via Shedhorn and the Duck Walk.

Although German forests tend to be managed by regular plantings, thinning, and clearing of debris, this woodsy area reminded people of Bavaria.

BEAR BACK / ●

This Pomalift, and the easy run beside it provides the residents of the Bighorn condos with ski in/ski out access. If you are nostalgic for midwestern skiing, a few laps on Bear Back will provide a cure.

Black bears have been seen wandering this area, and the hump between this and Silverknife resembles a bear's back. But anyone who has seen a rodeo and has bounced along with the Poma platter between their legs knows that it really should have been named for bare back bronc riding.

BEAR LAIR ♦

Entered through a gate near the top left of Bighorn, this glade run comes out on Bighorn in the flat bottoms. After the initial upper meadow, the trees get rather steep and tight. Several lines are available along the ridge and gully making for nice variations. The pitch and quantity of debris make this run best when there is good snow cover, but, in any case, this is one of the more difficult glades, requiring tight turns and good control.

In past years a bear has been known to hibernate in here, thus the name.

BIG COULOIR ♦ ♦

This is the closest Big Sky has to a "signature" run. At a 50 degree pitch and with over 1000 feet vertical drop it is one of the most intense in-bounds trails in America. Sign-out with the ski patrol and skiing with a partner; transceiver, probe, and shovel are required. Entry off the cornice is truly hair raising, but you are then

free to entertain the people at the top of the Triple chair and those in the Tram line with your skill and bravery.

Originally this was called "Schmitty's Couloir" after Brooks Heard's dog who did the first four legged descent on July 9, 1974. Schmitty did not create, nor was he responsible for, the frightening "dog leg" in the middle of the Couloir.

The term couloir means

Couloir and Gullies   *Glenniss Indreland*

16

passage or corridor in French. Others feel the derivation goes back to the French from the western term coulee that came from the verb couler to slip or slide. In either case you should ride or ski, but don't slip and slide down this narrow corridor.

BIG ROCK TONGUE ♦♦

Named before the Challenger lift was built; to ski this area, one had to hike from Upper Morningstar, traversing across Cache Trees, and up around to the front of Challenger. The rock tongues, big and little, were significant stony landmarks that you had to maneuver.

The Little Rock Tongue descents all have their own names now, but the Big Rock Tongue keeps its own. Too many words to say on a cold and windy day, the name has been shortened to BRT, pronounced Burrrt. BRT Main goes down the middle and one finds it by staying high up left on the ridge of the Highway. A ski patrol danger triangle sign leads to the entrance of a narrow rocky chute that opens to a steep, but lovely powder slope. Drop off the Highway to 17 Green and cut left to BRT South that descends on the right of BTR main, and you can avoid the rocky entrance of main. BRT North is a favorite double black. Descend Moonlight on your right to the trees. A narrow track can be found just below the exposed rocky talus slope on the right, keeping the trees to your left. Pick a careful line through the rocky cliff and you will find yourself on a sweet powder drop. All three BRT runs come out on Fast Lane for a return to the base area, or straight ahead to the Challenger lift and another great run.

True, steep double blacks, these runs require expert skill. Inbounds avalanches have occurred here.

BRT ROAD ■

Pronounced Burrrt by the locals this stands for Big Rock Tongue. This cat track road leads across the top of Lower Morningstar to the Challenger area and then continues on via Blue Moon to the Iron Horse lift, or via the Saddle Ridge Access to the Moonlight Lodge.

BIGHORN ■

Some skating along the wide path east from the top of Thunderwolf or straight off Ramcharger onto Ponderosa and a quick left on the cat track leads to Bighorn. One of the two main blue cruiser runs on the Thunderwolf side of Andesite, this run was named for *Ovis canadensis canadensis,* the Rocky Mountain Bighorn Sheep whose wide, thick, curved horn it resembles. You may be fortunate to see some of the local herd on the Spur Road, Lone Mountain Trail, just up from the stop light on US 191 where the West Fork crosses under the road.

There are many western places named for this beautiful animal. Among these are the Bighorn Mountains near Cody, WY and the Bighorn River that flows north to the

Bighorn Sheep near Big Sky
Travel Montana, Donnie Sexton

Yellowstone through the Crow reservation. The Bighorn condominiums near the Bear Back pomalift are named for Bighorn county in southeastern Montana with Hardin as the county seat. The Rocky Mountain Bighorn rams are noted for their sound-crashing head butting during the rut. Not to be confused with some boarder's behavior, this is discouraged between humans on this run.

A wide, beautifully groomed cruiser, this run is homologated, that is, measured and certified, by the FIS for international races in Downhill and Super G which are held here. But don't do this as a fast downhill. Savor the cruise, and stop to enjoy some of the loveliest views eastward to the Gallatin Canyon, Ramshorn Mountain, and the Gallatin Range.

BLACK AND BLUE ■

Not particularly difficult, this is an easy blue run left off of Lower Morningstar. However it only leads to the Challenger chairlift where all the runs are expert-only black and double black diamonds - thus black and blue.

If you do this run by mistake and are not an expert skier, there is a safe green exit on the Bozeman Trail that starts behind the Challenger lift loading station and ends up at the base area.

BLACK ROCK GULLY ♦

On the South Wall off the Turkey Traverse, this wide gully is named for the obvious large dark rock outcropping above the run.

Facing north, the runs off the South Wall are shaded until late in the year. This is not so good for visibility, but keeps the snow sweet.

BLACKFOOT ♦

Where Tippy's Tumble and Silverknife separate is a patch of deep woods with the sign for Blackfoot. Yes, indeed! You can ski in here. It is best in fresh deep snow. The trees are tight and it gets steep and stumpy at the bottom, making this the least desirable of the Andesite glades.

The Blackfoot are an Indian nation that, in historic times, occupied lands from near present day Edmonton, Alberta to the Yellowstone along the eastern front of the Rocky Mountains.

They were immortalized in the movie "Dances With Wolves" and the books such as James Willard Schultz's *My Life as an Indian* and *Fools Crow* by James Welch.

BLUE MOON ■

Moon from Moonlight and a blue square run make a perfect name for this cruiser to the Iron Horse lift. Going left off the Fast Lane, or right from BRT Traverse, this groomed and relatively flat run is easy to pick out among the bumps. It follows the valley and then angles to the left past the Diamond Hitch homes and down to the lift. It is the easiest of the runs off the Iron Horse.

It is the name of the Rogers & Hart 1933 song, "Blue moon/you saw me standing alone/without a dream in my heart/without a love of my own". This has been sung by many artists including Mel Torme, Elvis Presley, Bob Dylan, Eric

Clapton, and most famously by the Marcels. The song bridges all ages, and like this run, is great whatever your age.

BLUE ROOM ♦
Gondola II helped speed skiers up from the base area and was replaced with the Swiftcurrent high speed quad in 1996. One of the old blue square gondola cabins from this retired lift was hung deep in the trees near the top of this run where it served as a retreat and a smoke house - one of about 12 scattered about the resort. This is now gone, but it gave its name to the area and run. The gondola cabin was later replaced with a jerry-built shack of old boards and skis. You can question the symbolism, but this hut was squashed by a wind-blown tree that fell directly on it during the 2007 off-season. Like a phoenix, it has been resurrected and can be seen tucked in the trees skiers left as one enters off War Dance.

Blue Room, like its sister Coulter's Hell, tends to gather powder. Skiing in here can often be excellent even a day after the big dump when other runs have been skied off.

The run is a rather tight glade that is entered by going down War Dance to the first open meadow. Blue Room is directly to the left through the trees along the first 100 yards or so. It can also be entered through a gate in the trees off the upper right side of *Three Forks* just above Silverknife. Don't duck under the rope or you will find yourself going over, under and around deadfall.

The last third of the glade is rather steep with tight trees. This part can be avoided by taking the obvious road that reenters Silverknife.

BOB'S CORNER ♦
At the bottom of Dakota Bowl, way to the right side of Wyoming Bowl, is a left turn where the run goes east along a flat meadowed ridge to return to the bottom of the Dakota lift. This was named for Bob Dixon, a Big Sky ski patroller for 28 years, and now director of the ski patrol , who, along with Jon Ueland, explored this area back when it was out of bounds.

Bob tells of the early days skiing this when he kicked off a major avalanche here and was able to ski out of it.

MSU athletic logo, courtesy Montana State University, Bozeman

BOBCAT ♦
This run is named after *Lynx rufus* is a member of the cat family that is found in the Big Sky area. Rarely seen because of its nocturnal hunting habit, it is a very effective predator that feeds primarily on rabbits, mice, and other small mammals. The Bobcat is also the official mascot of the MSU (Montana State University) athletic teams.

A paired run with Grizzly Bear (the mascot of the rival University of Montana), this is the first left off Little Calf from the top of the Lone Moose lift. Nice bumps with an interesting series of pitches and varying fall lines make this a favorite run. It is lower than the rest of Big Sky, so has a problem with low snow and Spring melting weather. On the other hand, you need to take a road down from the base of the Thunderwolf lift to get to the runs on Flatiron Mountain, so it has no crowds and can be a source of fresh snow later on a powder day. Beware of the several ditches that are cut across this run.

BOLIVIA♦♦

Skier's right off War Dance can find you maneuvering through some tight trees to a small meadow that has the shape of Bolivia, the South American country. Opened as an official named run with a gate for the 2010-11 season, this steep, tight and difficult line leads into Marlboro Country and out Low Dog. It is only recommended if you have nothing else to do.

BONE CRUSHER ♦

This hiking area above the Swiftcurrent lift had a big avalanche in the early days that deposited huge blocks (bone crushers) of snow and ice debris. Fresh tracks can be had here, but it requires youthful legs and a ski patrol sign-out for the climb up.

BOOGER NUGGET ♦ a

Another name for *The Nose* off the end of the *Forested Knoll*, it gets its name from the permanent condition of patroller Jon "Yunce" Ueland's proboscis. It is a run as well as an avalanche path controlled to keep Never Sweat safe.

BOWL ♦

At one time, early on, this was called "Sunshine" Bowl, but the name never stuck. When you stand at the base of the Triple chair and look up you will see the Bowl with a bunch of lines named for rocks, the Big and Little Couloirs, the Gullies and the *Forested Knoll*. At this level on the mountain, what it looks like is what we call it.

Obviously named for the shape, this was our first black diamond run, and was one of only 18 runs present when Big Sky opened for its first season in 1974. Because it is so wide, it had a brief spell as a blue square run when Challenger, with its more difficult terrain, opened. However the pitch and the moguls that form here are much more difficult than the groomed blues like Calamity Jane or Ambush so it was returned to a black diamond to keep intermediates out of trouble.

This is great deep snow country, and, with access, could be skied as early as October, and well into May. Because the Bowl is so big and swings through more than 90 degrees of face, and because it is groomed by the wind that swirls up here; this unique area always has good lines somewhere on it. Wide open, it allows for long traverses for the intimidated. It also can provide a couple hours of enjoyment as you pick each of the several lines across the Bowl from *The Slot* to *Mary's Bush*. Try "shadow dancing" by following the edge of the Bonecrusher Ridge shadow as it moves across the open bowl on a sunny day.

Skiing the Bowl is a good test before trying Liberty Bowl. If you are not comfortable in the Bowl, you should not be skiing off the Tram.

BOZEMAN TRAIL ●

John Bozeman gained a bit of fame as a guide for wagon trains to the Montana gold fields over the trail he had found. It went north from the main Oregon trail and passed through Sioux country where the whites were not welcome and over the hill that I-90 takes between Livingston and Bozeman today. Bozeman was allegedly killed by these Indians (or perhaps a jealous husband) and the town was named for him.

This run is really a road and requires a bit of poling or skating to get down. It serves as the only easy outlet from the Challenger lift base for times when the lift is closed or for skiers who don't want to tackle the expert-only Challenger runs.

John Bozeman

BROKEN ARROW ◆

Many skiers arrows have been broken skiing this steep bit of moguls beneath the upper Thunderwolf chair. One of the original runs off the Mad Wolf chair, this run got a name with a western, Native American theme.

Broken Arrow was a movie and TV series that told a fictionalized account of the true historical relationship between Tom Jeffords, an Indian agent in Arizona, and the Chiricahua Apache chief Cochise.

BUFFALO JUMP ◆

Stay under the Swiftcurrent lift and go straight ahead just where Calamity Jane and Lobo veer off to the right. After the initial narrow, steep drop, a little left swing leads to a steep open slope down to a quasi- half pipe along a creek and back to Crazy Horse.

A buffalo jump is a cliff formation which Native Americans used for mass killings of bison. The animals were driven over the cliff where they were killed or injured then butchered by the waiting women. The Blackfeet word for this is "pishkun," which loosely translates as "deep blood kettle." Head-Smashed-In in southern Alberta, and the Ulm Pishkun and Madison Buffalo Jump in Montana are sites worth visiting. Hitting the start of this run at speed could end you up like the buffalo.

BUSH ◆

see *Mary's Bush*

BUTTRESS a

The Buttress is a large rock formation on the Little Rock Tongue between the Pinnacles and Cache Trees, and above the Gun Mount. Because of the location, it has an important avalanche path to control for the safety of the runs below.

21

CACHE TREES ♦ ♦

High on the side of the Little Rock Tongue, this run got its name as the place that the ski patrol cached a sled and rescue gear to use for injured skiers who had hiked into the Challenger area before the lift was installed.

Three very steep gladed descents are entered on the far right of Little Rock Tongue at the bottom of Country Club. You can catch the Cache Trees outrun by staying left on Upper Morningstar, through the rope gate and follow the traverse to the short, steep drops back down to Morningstar. These lines can be particularly good on powder days.

CALAMITY JANE ■

The favorite for intermediates from the top of the Swiftcurrent lift, this run parallels the Swiftcurrent lift in a series of hills and flats. Always well groomed, it is one of the first blues to try when you become confident on Mr. K.

Martha Jane Cannary Burke, better known as Calamity Jane (1852-1903), was a famous frontier figure of dubious reputation. Although she claimed that the name "Calamity" was given to her by a US Army captain after a disastrous Indian campaign, others say it came from the warning that men would "court calamity" if they offended her.

Calamity Jane 1895,

Indian fighter, prostitute, alcoholic, professional scout, and member of Buffalo Bill's Wild West Show; she is perhaps best known by her claim to have been Wild Bill Hickock's lover (which he denied). She is buried next to him in the Mt Moriah cemetery in Deadwood, S.D.

CARDIO TRIO ♦

This run, a black diamond through the trees of the Bavarian Forest, follows the Dakota lift line. It was named in honor of the Big Sky Cardiology Conference whose doctors have been coming to Big Sky since 1978. Founded by Dr. Sid Goldstein, Dr. Dan Anbe, and Dr. Phil Hill, the run was named in 2008 to commemorate the group's 30th anniversary at Big Sky.

Cardio refers to "heart" for the conference and also for cardiovascular, or aerobic exercise. This type of exercise increases your heart rate - a definite result of this run.

CASCADE /

The real estate access lift to the Cascade subdivision opened in 2003. This explains why there is a lift going over the road between Big Sky and Moonlight, as skiing on the roads around here is discouraged.

A cascade is a waterfall descending over a steep rocky surface. The name of this subdivision comes from Cascade County with Great Falls as its seat. The county's name comes from the nearby falls on the Missouri River that became famous for its long delay of Lewis & Clark's Corps of Discovery in 1804.

CASTRO'S ♦ ♦

The steepest named run on the mountain's trail map at 51 degrees, this run is to the right of Lenin and the Dictators. People with a good imagination looking up can see all of this old Cuban's features; the forehead, nose, beard; all of which describe lines of descent.

CHALLENGER /

Installed in 1988 in the area that had long been called Challenger by hikers, the lift added much needed expert terrain to the original Big Sky acreage. By pure coincidence, the tragic Challenger space shuttle explosion occurred at the time of the lift installation.

CHALLENGER LIFT LINE ♦

Follow Fast Lane to where the Challenger chair passes over and you can descend the moguls along this lift line to the base of this lift. Somewhat narrow, and with lift towers to avoid, the pitch is moderate. There is no official name for this run that is used mostly by the tourists.

CHALLENGER TREES ♦

Locals named this section of Magic Meadows where it parallels the Challenger lift. A drop into the trees just as BRT Traverse takes the big left turn to the Challenger area, or off the Fast Lane just past the lift line, will lead to a lovely set of trees and small open areas. Tight, but of moderate pitch, this is rarely skied, so often has good snow. It exits onto the Challenger Lift Line at the flat run-out to the lift.

CHAMBER POT a

This avalanche path goes down a bowl of snow off the summit and just east of the Tram . It is not open nor skiable, but if you were foolish enough to get in to it, please note that it ends on a steep rock cliff and you will be deep into the contents of a chamber pot.

CHET'S KNOB●

This green bump at the end of Lone Wolf and next to the Explorer chair gives a little pitch before ending at the Explorer chair or the base area. It was formerly

called Nastar Knob for the Nastar racecourse that previously was set here and whose starter hut remains. The snowcat packer drivers called it Chet's Knob because they could see directly into Chet's Bar in the Huntley Lodge from here. That name has been formally adopted to honor the founder of this resort.

Looking east from Chet's knob   Glenniss Indreland

CHIPPEWA NOTCH ♦

To the right of Wyoming Bowl, far right in Dakota Territory, this area was named by Todd Amble, a patroller with Minnesota connections. Famous in that state for its casinos and wild rice, this tribe has no connection to Montana or Big Sky.

CHUCK'S RUN ■

To get to this run that is a bit off the beaten path, you will need to bear to the right just above the spot where Lobo Meadows enters the obvious valley. A sign marks the way, but you will need to keep speed as the track goes uphill a bit before coming on the run. Rarely groomed, there can be fresh tracks late on a powder day. These "freshies" are your reward for enduring the long cat track return along Middle Road. The big powder bump to your right as you approach Chuck's Run, can be reached by a secret walk through the woods off Cow Flats at the junction with Lobo Meadows. A little work, but rewarded with a couple of nice powder turns.

There were many local Chucks who have been reputed to be the source of this name. Among them are Chuck Seymour, one of the original American ski instructors at Big Sky, and Chuck Anceny, a legend who passed away in 2009 and whose family goes back to the early 1900s in Gallatin Gateway and Big Sky. However, the real "Chuck" of this run was Chuck Moll, Everett Kircher's right hand man. Not warm and fuzzy, he was a hard driving businessman who was responsible for seeing that Mr. Kircher's orders were carried out.

COUNTRY CLUB ♦

Up above the Highway, this was part of the hiking route before the Challenger lift.

Wide open and mellow, and looking rather like a golf course, this is the field you see to your left as you come to the top of the Challenger lift. Easy itself, it leads to some serious steep off the Little Rock Tongue - like the Pinnacles, Cache Trees, Little Tree, Onslow's, and the Zucchini Patch. The easiest way down is to enjoy the open, but hang left above the trees, traversing past the dead trees and on to descend the Highway to BRT Traverse or Lower Morningstar.

COW FLATS ■

More of a cat track than a run, this easy route is the way to get to the Shedhorn lift and runs from the Swiftcurrent side. It is a blue square only because there are no green runs on Shedhorn. The first right turn off Lobo or Lobo Meadows gets you there and is well signed. Cow Flats also collects the exits from Paradise, Packsaddle, Dude Park, and Yellow Mule before reaching the base of the Shedhorn lift. Be sure to maintain good speed as there are flat areas, and no respectable skier should be seen walking. Also, be sure to go straight across the Middle Road or you will take a long slow trip back to the base area.

The loggers that cut the runs at Shedhorn also did the Iron Horse area, and this access trail from the Swiftcurrent side ended up flat enough "to herd cows". It has never been known to be an actual grazing area.

COLTER'S HELL ♦

John Colter (c: 1774-1812) was a member of the Lewis and Clark expedition and one of the first mountain men. He explored the area around present day Yellowstone and Grand Teton National Parks, so may have been the first white man in Big Sky. His stories of geysers, mud pots and steaming vents was ridiculed as fantasy - thus the nickname "Colter's Hell" for Yellowstone.

This glade is anything but Hell. It is a black diamond glade, but relatively well spaced trees and a north face that tends to hold good snow make for a lovely run. Take the gate into War Dance off the *Three Forks* and follow this to where it opens up onto a meadow with little trees. Colter's Hell parallels War Dance in the trees to the lower left. Enter the trees too early and you will find yourself in the Blue Room. The run comes out on a road where a left returns to the base area and Ramcharger, and a right goes down the Mineshaft of War Dance to the Low Dog trail to Thunderwolf.

CONGO ♦

When this glade was cleared, a name was needed to go with Africa and Safari. Although conjuring images of deep, dark jungles, this short glade has a steady pitch and is nicely thinned. Clearly a black diamond, because of the trees, and moguls, this is the shortest and easiest of the Andesite glades and the first you should try if you want to learn to ski trees.

A whole series of entrance lines are available as one cruises along Safari. Left, right, or center, all the lines are good. Take a peek, there is no harm in looking. This is what a glade is supposed to be like. If it appears too tight for you, just continue along Safari to meet your party again as they emerge from the trees of the Congo.

CRAZY HORSE ■

Straight ahead behind the Triple chair base, and to the right of Mr. K are the series of hills and flats of Crazy Horse. Not particularly difficult terrain, this run is less often groomed than Calamity Jane or Lobo, and tends to develop easy moguls. Be sure to keep speed on the flat areas to avoid a walk.

Crazy Horse (1840-1877) was a Hunkpapa Sioux and their premier war chief. He led their victory over General Custer at the Battle of the Little Big Horn. His war cry of, "It is a good day to fight. It is a good day to die!" encompasses his spirit. He never surrendered, and never signed a treaty. He was murdered at Fort Robinson where he went under safe conduct to see his wife who was dying of tuberculosis. There is no recorded photograph of this man so the mountain being carved in South Dakota is an idealization.

CRAZY RAVEN ♦

Named by John Kircher, son of Boyne scion, Everett Kircher, John was the third General Manager of Big Sky where he served from 1984-97. When this run was being cut, the resident flock of ravens gathered and were busy snatching the workers' lunches. The name of the run fits with the Native American sounding theme as well as the "Mad" theme of Mad Wolf which it parallels.

In the early days, this was not a cleared run and had lots of trees and deadfall. Although it has now been opened up considerably, it still tends to be steep with big moguls. It runs right of Broken Arrow with multiple exits to that run on skier's left. The narrow bottom of this run can be fun with challenging Volkswagen sized moguls, but it gets a bit rocky. In low snow times an earlier exit to Broken Arrow is prudent.

CRON'S ♦♦

The traverse to the left out of the First Gully midway down crosses the ridge and comes down Cron's into the Cue Ball below the Big Couloir. A black diamond, it was originally accessed by hiking up the ridge above the Triple chair. As it now is now entered from the double black Gullies, some caution is advised. This is particularly good as a way out of the Gullies when their lower section gets rocky. It also is one of the areas used for the Powder Eights competition, so good turns can be had on this wall.

It was named for Bob Cron, who was the Squaw Creek ranger in the 70s. The upper part of Big Sky was in his US Forest Service jurisdiction at that time, and since he was the supervisor here, he necessarily had to "inspect". With the land exchange in 1983 that brought upper Big Sky into private Boyne USA ownership, the Forest Service no longer needed a supervisor here. Bob became the Bozeman ranger when the Squaw Creek (now Storm Castle Creek) district of the Gallatin National Forest merged with it. He later went on to be a supervisor in Washington state, and has retired to western Colorado.

CUE BALL ♦♦

Cron's and the Big Couloir both enter into this slide path that is very visible from the top of the Triple Chair and the Tram line. It is said to look just like a pool cue ball from the air.

Although easy itself, the only runs that enter this area are double blacks.

DAKOTA BOWL/ GULLY/TREES/TRAIL ♦

Originally an out of bounds area, ski patroller Younce and friends called it Dakota Territory because it looked flat. Dakota Bowl is very steep from the top gate off the ridge on Liberty Bowl. However, skiing it from the top of the Dakota lift to the open Bowl and the Forest runs finds a pitch about like Africa. The trees and the remote nature of the area give it the black diamond.

This area has been skied since the Tram gave access to Liberty Bowl with lines down Dakota Bowl or the Bavarian Forest. With the addition of the Dakota lift in 2007 the gully and trees were thinned making for some mellow black diamond skiing. It faces south, so can melt soft sooner, but the distance from the base area keeps the crowds away.

Access off Liberty Bowl is through a series of gates. The first, is found by following the ridge at the top of Liberty to the southern roped corner. It leads into out of bounds skiing at the top of the Dakota Bowl where steep, deep powder can be found. This is also a high avalanche danger area, and, as it is out of bounds, it is not cleared by the ski patrol. Ski it with caution, a buddy, and your transceiver, probe and shovel. The second gate through the ropes, is partway down Liberty and enters the bowl below the steeper section. This, too is out of bounds so enter at your own risk. The main gate, with a wooden arch and sign is at the bottom of Liberty Bowl where it meets the first trees. This is just above the top of the Dakota lift, and enters a groomed track that leads to the top of the Dakota lift and all of the runs in the area. The Dakota Territory can also be reached via the Mule Skinner cat track from the top of the Shedhorn lift to the bottom of Dakota lift. It is the only black diamond track on the mountain for a reason. It is much nicer to enter through Liberty Bowl.

You may notice many dead or dying trees here. When the lift was put in in 2007, the forest was very healthy. However the triple assault of a white pine blister rust, pine beetle, and a general warming have devastated the Whitebark pine forests throughout the Rocky Mountains. The Dakota Territory is one of Lone Mountain's hardest hit areas.

DEAD TOP ♦ a

This steep area on the Little Rock Tongue can be found by staying left on Upper Morningstar through the roped gate and traversing the ridge that parallels Gun Mount. Short, but often with serious powder, it adds a bit of excitement to the trip to the base or Challenger from the Triple.

It was named for a dead tree that helps define an avalanche route.

DEEP SOUTH●

With the position as the farthest south of the runs on Southern Comfort, the name was obvious. As with Southern Comfort area itself, the run was named to recognize the many regular ski club visitors from the deep south; Florida, Alabama, Georgia, and the Carolinas particularly.

From the Ramcharger lift take the *Yellow Brick Road* to the right off the top of Ponderosa and follow it across Eldorado and Sacajawea to Deep South. Or if you start from the top of the Southern Comfort lift, turn left where Sacajawea and Deep South run together. Sacajawea turns left first, so keep going on this nice smooth green.

About 3/4 of the way down is an entrance gate access on your right to the Yellowstone Club. This gate house is manned, and access is by invitation only. You don't want to go there anyway, so continue on your merry way.

Where Sacajawea rejoins this run, there is a flattish run-out. In the middle is a spring that can be quite icy or wet in low snow times. The ski patrol ropes off the spring, and this is done for a reason. Pass on either side of the ropes lest you find yourself riding on parts of your body that weren't meant to be skied on.

DICTATORS ♦ ♦

In the days before the Tram, skiers would hike up across the top of the Gullies and around over Marx and Lenin, who were so steep they had to be really bad dudes. Castro was beyond, named because it looked like his profile, so the chutes in between had to also be... dictators.

Down the steep roller on the right side of Lenin then to the right to take the top or middle traverse to these steep, narrow chutes. Enjoy!

DIRTBAG WALL ♦ ♦

Dirtbags are a modern slang term for ski bums, people who are a bit more interested in skiing than employment or personal appearance. Big Sky has an annual Dirtbag Ball where a yearly king, queen, and court are crowned and skiing and partying are celebrated. Dirtbags and wannabees can be seen the day of the ball all over the mountain in outrageous costume.

The dirtbag tree on the right of the Swiftcurrent lift is festooned with Mardi Gras beads and undergarments of large proportion in celebration of the free spirit. On the lift ride, a local grandfather was explaining to his young grandson why there was all that underwear in this tree. It took all the rest of the day for the grandfather to convince the young fellow that he should not put his Spiderman underpants in the tree as well.

This steep wall is accessed by staying high on the left side of Marx and crossing the ridge at the little sign. A whole series of chutes descend to the Duck Walk. These are named for the Dirtbag Royalty: Ace, King, Queen, Jack, Wild Card as well as Wall Chute, and S-curve, or Bobsled.

UPPER DOBE'S a, DOBE'S ♦ ♦ AND DOBE'S EXIT♦ ♦

Directly under the Tram, and to skier's right of the Big Couloir and the Chamber Pot, these exceptionally steep walls are skiable now only by hiking up. Upper Dobe's is an avalanche path that has reportedly been skied only once. The entry to the rest, over the cliffs from the Gullies, is extremely dangerous and has been closed. The twenty foot rock cliff between Dobe's Exit and Dobe's adds further hazard to this very extreme route.

Dobe was a member of the original survey crew that mapped the mountain for runs in 1974. He subsequently went into the Forest Service and has since retired to Idaho.

DUCK WALK ■

This cat track from the top of the Shedhorn lift takes skiers back to the top of the Swiftcurrent lift where it continues on as the Jay Walk. In addition to people coming up the Shedhorn lift, it collects skiers from Lenin, Marx, and the Dirtbag Wall for their return to the Tram or the base. Off to the right one can drop down into Yellow Mule, upper Dude Park, Packsaddle and Paradise from this track.

It was named the Duck Walk by patroller Eddie Garcia in honor of Bob Dixon, the current Ski Patrol Director. Bob's radio code name is "Red Duck Leader" apparently because, although he can ski like a dream, he is reputed to walk like a duck.

DUDE PARK ♦

Although western in sound, for the well dressed easterner unfamiliar with the cowboy way, that is not where the name comes from. It is a nod to the snowboarder culture who adopted the word in reference to an individual. This big powder field, as with most of Shedhorn, has become a magnet for boarders.

Upper Dude Park runs through the open area to the left of the Shedhorn lift and Yellow Mule. The choice part of the run, however, is best found by going

28

down Yellow Mule and taking a left along the Middle Road. After a couple hundred yards, big pillowy mounds and wide spaced trees appear for a real powder feast.

ELDORADO ●

The mythical city of gold gave its name to several rich mining districts in the West. This wide open, easy run under the Southern Comfort lift is an Eldorado for the beginner.

The access as the first run to the left off the *Yellow Brick Road,* or directly from the Southern Comfort lift, finds this great practice slope. Beginners can sweep back and forth on the wide groomed part, novice shredders try the powder in the small trees of Fremont's Forest on the right, lift riders holler at their friends; everyone has a good time on this run.

ELK PARK ■ RIDGE AND MEADOWS■

"Park" refers to a natural open meadow in the mountains. Much of this ridge was a natural open park and before, and, even after the ski runs were cut, this magnificent animal could be found grazing in this area. Elk, *Cervus canadensis,* is also called the Wapiti. This member of the deer family is common in the Big Sky area and herds can occasionally be seen on the golf course. Large numbers in the Gallatin herd are often seen on the hillsides east of the Gallatin River just south of Big Sky.

For one of the premier cruiser runs in the country, just take the first right off *Three Forks* at the end of the Andesite cat track. The gentle rolls and a consistent pitch that seems to go on forever make this a favorite. It is a great first choice for stepping up to the blues, and the views don't hurt either.

Madison Avenue starts from this run, but the sweetest alternate to the Ridge itself is the Meadows, the ungroomed open area all along the right of the ridge. Wide open, rolling and of a modest pitch, this can be a great place to practice your first off piste powder.

Cervus canadiensis   *Mongo*

END OF THE WORLD a

This connotes the rock wall that is between the Big and Little Couloirs. It is not even considered a true avalanche path as it is too steep to hold snow.

ERICA'S GLADE ♦

Off the end of the ridge above the right of Screaming Left at the bottom of Liberty Bowl is a little wooden sign that leads into the woods and out onto Aspen Meadows. The trees are Erica's Glade. Named in honor of Erica Pankow, it was her favorite run.

29

Christmas of 1996 saw a huge dump of snow, and Erica was patrolling with a partner off the Tram. She was doing avalanche mitigation work when the charge exploded, killing her instantly.

Please enjoy the beauty of this glade in her memory.

EVERETT'S ANGER ♦

This lower straight section of the Rock Pocket was cut when John Kircher was GM of Big Sky. The name comes from his father's opinion of the run. Good bumps, good pitch, good snow.

EXIT CHUTE ♦ ♦

At the far end of the Turkey Traverse along the South Wall, is the last chute to get off the Wall. It is short, but quite steep, and maneuvers through the rocks at this end of the Wall.

EXPLORER /

This chair has been in operation since the resort opened in 1974. It serves the beginner runs in front of the Huntley Lodge.

FAST LANE ■

Named because it is the direct route back to the Base Area from the Challenger and Iron Horse, it has a fairly fast descent for a track, thus the blue square.

It receives skiers from the cliff area of Outer Limits, Midnight Trees, Moonlight, BRT and 17 Green. It also serves as the entrance to Bad Dog, Challenger Lift Line, and Black and Blue. After it crosses Lower Morningstar it heads up a hill to Mr. K. This can be made with speed and herringbone, but the wise older skier turns left on Morningstar for a more leisurely run to the base. I mean, it's not that Mr. K is so spectacular that you should grunt to the top of that hill.

FERAL ●

This newly named area winds right of the small new growth pines on the south side of Eldorado.

A feral animal is one that has escaped domestication and returned to a more or less wild state. Do I hear you thinking, "snowboarder"?

FLAT IRON MOUNTAIN

This is the name of the mountain, actually a ridge, off Andesite, that contains the Lone Moose lift and runs. Named for the shape by the local developer, the official USGS Flatiron Mountain in Montana is west of US 287 and the Madison Valley, near Wade Lake.

FORESTED KNOLL ♦ a

The knob to the right of the Lone Peak Triple chair as you are going up is called *The Forested Knoll*. The only area with trees in the Bowl, it tends to hold its powder and has some nice steep drops. Watch out for exposed rocks. *Tower 10* which drops into the Bowl, and *The Nose,* or *"Booger Nugget"* into Never Sweat are the two main lines. Both are unofficially named as runs and are avalanche paths as well.

FREEMONT'S FOREST●

Freemont is the big moose mascot for the SnowSports School. You may be fortunate (?) enough to see him in the base area and get a bug fuzzy hug or have your picture taken with him.

This newly named run has just been opened for the 2010-11 season. It winds through the small new growth pines on the right side of Eldorado, giving a first, and relatively safe glade adventure to the young green skiers and boarders. No big hard trunks, and the branches are soft when you hit them, just don't trip!

GONDOLA SHAFT ♦

Dropping off the Jay Walk into the area where the old Gondola I house stood, this short run gets you to the cat track to the Rice Bowl.

GREAT WHITE ♦

A short steep drop from where the Jay Walk takes its wide left turn, goes to the old road above the Rice Bowl. Ropes often are placed to prevent skiers from breaking on the rocky parts, but the entrance gates lead to nice lines. As an aside, this roped place on the Jay Walk is a good spot to take photos with Lone Peak in the background.

Although rocky in times of low snow due to the pitch, it can be loaded with snow. It is not clear if the name comes from the load of white snow, or from the rocks that look like great white shark's teeth, ready to eat you.

GRIM REAPER a

This avalanche path lies to the right of Cache Trees as you are looking up the Little Rock Tongue. It is notorious for breaking off a big slow moving slab every two to three years. Thus the name.

GRIZZLY BEAR ♦

Ursus arctos horribilis, the grizzly bear is the largest carnivore in the Yellowstone ecosystem and not infrequently seen near Big Sky.

The Grizzly is also the official mascot of the UM (University of Montana) sports teams. The rivalry with the MSU Bobcats necessitated, for safety reasons, separating the two runs by the Lone Moose Lift.

Take Little Calf to the obvious signed entrance on your left. The run is a set of straight steep walls to test your bump technique.

Griz logo, used with permission of the University of Montana

GUILFORD'S LADDER ●

This cutoff to the skier's left off Mr. K goes to Lone Wolf and on to the Ski Patrol and First Aid house and Clinic.

It was named for Curtis Guilford, a long time operations employee, after his death from heart disease.

GULLIES ♦ ♦ a

See image under Big Couloir

Named obviously, because they are steep gullies that come off Bonecrusher ridge above the Bowl.

This is an important area for control of the avalanches that can come down into the Bowl and Turkey Traverse. Gullies 1, 2, and 3 are the most skiable, but the avalanche control continues the numbering to 4, 5, and 6 followed by Tits Up and the Waterfall. The latter is best done like Niagara Falls... in a barrel... with similar results. These runs are approached via a track, the Gullies Traverse, on the left of Marx a short way down. They have a very steep exposure and get quite narrow through the rock band halfway down. During early season snow, when they are particularly tight and rocky, it is best to cut across the short track, skiers left of the 1st Gully, to Cron's for the descent back to the Tram line. If you are not comfortable skiing Marx and Lenin you should stay away from the Gullies.

GUN MOUNT ♦

Heading straight off Upper Morningstar will take you off the toe of the Lone Peak rock glacier. This is a nice, moderately steep short run, often with good powder, that goes directly onto Lower Morningstar bypassing the cat track and the flats around the Triple chair.

It is named for the US Army recoilless rifle that had a platform near here. This was used for shooting avalanches in the Bowl area and was replaced with the Avalauncher that is now housed farther up on Upper Morningstar. With the land exchange in 1983 this cannon was removed, because the land in the Bowl became private Boyne property and the Army will only shoot its ordinance on Federal land.

The Avalauncher, used now, a two-chambered pneumatic (compressed gas) cannon, is probably the most popular civilian weapon in use. The trajectory is varied by altering the firing angle and the nitrogen pressure.

HANGING VALLEY ♦ ♦

Under the Kircher Cliffs to the right of the Dakota Bowl, this area can have wonderful powder. It also can be quite unstable. This is the place where John Kircher was caught in the avalanche that gave the cliffs their name. He was able to ski out of it and was unhurt.

HANGMAN'S ■

Directly down from the top of the Ramcharger lift and a little left is Hangman's.

It is frequently roped off when it is used for racing as it has been Homologated as an official FIS Slalom/Giant Slalom course. Homologation by the FIS is where a course is measured, recorded, and certified for international racing. Practice your short slalom turns on the narrow ridge to the right, or your GS technique down the wider left and center.

The name comes as a result of the romantic, western theme and the Vigilantes who were active in our Madison County during the gold rush of the 1860's. It also comes from the fact that if you hit the roller about 2/3 of the way down at speed, you could end hanging yourself in the trees.

HIGH CLEARING ♦

Named for the location, this open steep lies just to the right of the Highway and left of the Zucchini Patch. After dropping down the opening between the groves of trees, it enters the Highway a bit above the BRT Traverse, or you hang right along the ridge and into the Zucchini Patch.

Quite a bit steeper than the Highway, this is a good place to practice the steeps after you have mastered the pitch of the Highway.

HIGHWAY ♦

Before the Challenger lift was installed, people would ski this area by traversing across from the top of the Triple Chair and around the Little Rock Tongue. They would then angle up on a line that looked like a "highway". Since it is also big and wide open, the name stuck .

The run cruises along the ridge and small trees at the top of Challenger following the lift line, then turns right, downhill, to a wide set of bumps to the BRT traverse and Lower Morningstar. Although it looks like the easiest way down, the lower section is south facing. As a result the snow conditions tend towards crud and ice. In good conditions, especially on a sunny afternoon, this can be sweet. However, conditions are often better going down 17 Green or Moonlight to the Fast Lane.

HIPPY HIGHWAY ■

Coming off the bottom of the Bavarian Forest and Erica's Glade. this feeder track passes along the bottom of Sunlight to the Shedhorn Lift. Before the Dakota lift was built, it was the only return from Dakota Territory, and was named for the young and crazy that would frequent these runs.

HUNTLEY HOLLOW ■
HUNTLEY LODGE

This easier exit, a mellow blue, is straight ahead off the bottom of Calamity Jane. It was named for Chet Huntley, newscaster at NBC, who's dream of a ski resort in Montana became the reality of Big Sky Resort.

Chester Robert Chet Huntley (12/10/1911-3/20/1974) was born in

Chet Huntley (R)   *Boyne USA archives*

33

nearby Cardwell, MT just off I-90, some 50 miles west of Bozeman, and attended Montana State. He went on to fame as a news anchor on NBC with David Brinkley from 1956 to 1970. He served as spokesman, and a minority partner of the consortium that started Big Sky and that eventually sold to the Boyne Corporation, the present owner. Chet Huntley died of lung cancer at his Big Sky home before the resort opened, but his image and plans for Big Sky continue to this day. Good night, Chet

IN RUN, LUNCH BOX a
An avalanche path off the rocks above the Low Bench is not for skiing; but it is important to control slides into the Bowl area.

IRON MAIDEN ♦
An iron maiden is a torture device, consisting of an iron cabinet, with a hinged front, rather like a mummy case. It usually has a small closeable opening so that the torturer can interrogate the victim and can torture or kill him by using holes made for knives, spikes or nails.

The run descends along a narrow, mogully pitch under the Iron Horse lift, ending at the Saddle Ridge access trail to Moonlight Lodge. Stumps, rocks and narrow , this can be torture. However, with deep, fresh snow, she can be a very sweet maiden

IRON HORSE /
This lift installed 1994 comes from the translation of the Indian name for a locomotive. It was installed by the Moonlight Basin folks when it was the pattern for developers to place the lift and have Big Sky manage the skiing. When Moonlight Basin decided to open its own ski resort, it reverted back to them while also remaining part of the Big Sky system. Now, with "The Biggest Skiing in America", it provides a joint interconnection to these two great resorts and allows skiers access to 5500 acres of fun.

JAY WALK ●
This cat track from the top of the Swiftcurrent chair to the Triple and the entrance to Mr K, Lower Morningstar, and Crazy Horse is an extension of the Duck Walk. Continuing further on across the top of Lower Morningstar, it will extend into BRT Traverse, which goes across the Challenger runs, and eventually to Moonlight Lodge.

Because a separate name was needed to define this area, and because patroller Jay Frisque did something infamous, but still anonymous, here, it was named for him.

JOCK STRAP ♦
Because the bottom end of Larkspur was often closed as unskiable, this run was cut to provide an exit to Larkspur. With its shape, and because it protects from lower Larkspur, known as *Ball Buster*, the name seemed appropriate.

Really just a narrow road cut from a hillside, this tends to get bumpy and scraped rocky. However, with first powder tracks, it is a delight.

34

KEYHOLE ♦

This nice little powder stash in the woods is accessed via a tight, winding trail that starts to the skier's left near the top of the Stump Farm. A fast down off the first drop on Stump Farm is followed by a sharp uphill left into the trees and a wander through the woods that leads to this nice open glade and powder field that ends on the Middle Road.

Named for its shape, keyholes are tiny little things that are hard to get through. But, it's what is on the other side of the door... Yes!

KIRCHER'S CLIFFS

This was named for John Kircher, son of Boyne founder, Everett Kircher, and general manager of Big Sky from 1980-96. In 1994, he was skiing with Patrollers Bob Dixon, Jon Ueland, and future GM, Taylor Middleton. They had helicoptered to the peak to scout the area to be served by the new Tram, and were on the cliffs above the Hanging Valley when John took "a little ride". It was not a serious avalanche, he was able to ski out of it and was not buried, so the cliffs were named in his honor.

John Kircher (R) at Tram construction
Glenniss Indreland

These cliffs are on US Forest Service property and can develop quite a cornice. The government has not as yet given permission for the ski patrol to set charges in this area for avalanche control. This is why the Dakota Bowl and the more western areas like the Hanging Valley are sometimes closed. The results of huge avalanches have been seen here, so please observe the closure signs and ropes as they are put up at times of significant danger.

LARKSPUR ♦

Larkspur is a wild Delphinium that is common in the area around Lone Peak. It is to be wondered why the Big Sky people named this gnarly run that ends up on the Jockstrap for this beautiful, delicate wild flower. On the other hand, Delphinium does produce a deadly toxic cardiac glycoside. Hmmmm... watch where you ski.

The run is a series of interconnecting trails that wind under and next to the Shedhorn lift. Starting on Yellow Mule, turning right; going directly under the lift; or following the powder in the open talus field and bearing to the left of Sunlight, all eventually bring you to Jock Strap and the base of the lift.

Delphinium grandiflora, Sydenham Edwards,

35

LENIN ♦ ♦

V. I. Lenin

Marx and Lenin were named that by the locals who hiked up to ski them before the Tram was built. It was during the Cold War, and along with Castro, they seemed like really bad dudes. When the Tram was completed, the sales and marketing people wanted to call them Thunder and Lightening causing an outcry. Lenin and Marx - L M for Lone Mountain - won out and that is what we are skiing today.

The first run you come to on the Yeti Traverse, Lenin is steep, but very consistent, and usually has excellent snow. Watch for the big rock middle right at the bottom of the first narrow section. The easiest line is on the left side at the start of the bowl, and the shoulder on the right is steeper, but exciting. The short traverses to the Dictator Chutes are off to the upper right of this part of the run. At the bottom, as Lenin flattens towards the Duck Walk, conditions can sometimes get lumpy as chicken heads and death cookies form. It is often better to take the short traverse to the left over the rocky ridge to the bottom of Marx to finish the descent.

LIBERTY BOWL ♦

This is the easiest, albeit by no means easy, way off the summit. Following the green dots on sticks will get you to the bottom with the least trauma. Rocks tend to sprout up at the top right, but below the snow fences the whole expanse is skiable. This bowl also provides access to the Yeti Traverse, Dakota Bowl, Erica's Glade, the Bavarian Forest, and Aspen Meadows. Although it is the easiest route off the summit, it is a long, steep black diamond. Do not try this run if you are not comfortable skiing the Bowl.

If you are into skiing the longest continuous run on the mountain, you can go from Liberty Bowl to the Base Area via Middle Road - 6 miles. Recommended only for people interested in records this follows one of the steeper routes on Liberty, and one of the flattest and slowest along the Middle Road.

Before the Tram, this run was reached by an all day climb from the Bowl, and, because it was so far, so cold, and so windy, with no easy return, it was known as Siberia. It was briefly called Stutzman's Bowl in honor of David Stutzman, who was killed in an avalanche on Andesite in 1983, but became Liberty Bowl as a happier alternative to Marx, Lenin and the Dictators after the Tram arrived.

LITTLE CALF ●

The green easy way down from the top of the Lone Moose lift fit with the "little" theme on this side of the mountain. Flat, wide and gentle, it has a faintly Native American ring, but no actual Indian reference.

Calves are the young of domestic cattle, so this route avoids the herd of adult skiers and boarders going down Bobcat or Grizzly. As easy as this run is to negotiate, no one needs worry about becoming veal.

LITTLE COULOIR ♦ ♦
See image on Big Couloir

A bit west or left of the Big Couloir, it is steeper and narrower that the Big Couloir with a pitch between 50 and 55 degrees. It is usually only skiable in good snow years as the pitch doesn't hold snow

As with the Big Couloir, you will need permission from the ski patrol and sign out to try this run.

LITTLE DOGIE ●
In the Old West, a motherless or small, runty calf was sometimes referred to as a dogie. In the cowboy ballad, Dogie's Lament also known as Git Along Little Dogie, the "dogies" in question were cattle strong enough to handle a cattle drive, and not just calves or orphans. The name fits again with the "little" theme as it runs into Little Calf.

This flat green run comes off the top of the Lone Moose lift and makes the easy return to Bighorn and the Thunderwolf lift.

Taking this run hardly leads to "your misfortune and none of my own".

LITTLE EWE●
Below the Bighorn headwall, this gentle, wide run angles right to take you to the Southern Comfort lift, which can be seen from the entrance to this run. For skiers intimidated by the pitch of Bighorn, this makes a nice escape to the easier area on Andesite Mountain.

Ewe refers to the docile adult female sheep. Not wanting you to be a dumb domestic animal, and coming off Bighorn run, it must be believed that the name refers to the female of the Rocky Mountain Bighorn Sheep. Hopefully you will have seen our local herd that are frequently found by the Spur Road, Lone Mountain Trail, just up from the entrance to Big Sky.

It is not to be worried that in both ancient and modern religious ritual, sheep are used as sacrificial animals.

LITTLE GULLIES ♦ ♦
These steep, narrow gullies come off the LRT Traverse between Cache Trees and Little Tree. They are very difficult and best skied with good snow cover.

LITTLE MUSSOLINI ♦ ♦
A steep route down the right side of Lenin and to the left of the First Dictator is characterized by a distinctive rock at its top.

Mussolini, Il Duce, was the dictator of Italy before and during the Second World War. He was killed by a mob and his body was dragged beaten and bloody through the streets. Not that this allusion has anything to do with you or this run...

Benito Mussolini, G. G. Bain

37

LITTLE ROCK TONGUE ♦♦

The Little Rock Tongue is the prominent outcropping on the Challenger that had to be negotiated when hiking to this area before the lift went in. The run refers to that part of the slope below Country Club that leads into Little Tree, Cache Trees, Little Gullies and the Zucchini Patch. These are all steep, narrow double black diamonds. It these appear too steep for your comfort, just go left above the trees to the Low Clearing or Highway.

LITTLE THUNDER ●/

The original roads in Big Sky were named for historic Native American people. The road served by this lift and access run is called Little Thunder.

It is a common Lakota surname seen today, but the historic chief lived ca. 1820-1879. He was a leader of the Brule band of Lakota (Sioux) and known for his efforts to compromise with the whites. His band was the victim of the Grattan Massacre by the US Army in 1855.

Little Thunder

LITTLE TREE ♦♦

This is a steep, narrow run off the bottom of Country Club and Little Rock Tongue. The entrance is noted by a small, solitary pine tree that is easy to see and marks the top of the run. It exits into the fan leading to Lower Morningstar.

LOBO ■ LOBO MEADOWS■

Lobo is Spanish for wolf, especially the Mexican wolf, *Canis lupus baileyi*. Wolves have been reintroduced into the Yellowstone ecosystem in recent years, and have occasionally been sighted in our community. But even before this reintroduction, there were wolves at Big Sky with our runs of Lobo, Lone Wolf and Mad Wolf.

Lobo is a lovely cruiser with some nice headwalls that starts with Calamity Jane directly off the Swiftcurrent lift, then angles right. Not as frequently groomed as Calamity Jane, Lobo can have some nice snow if skied early on a powder day. There is a natural spring on the right side on the top of the last headwall - right after Lobo Meadows re-enters. Watch for the bamboo markers as this can leave you howling.

For a little more adventure, Lobo Meadows is rarely groomed and starts to the right of the lift, passing through a set of moguls before turning left over some rollers to rejoin Lobo at its midway.

LONE MOOSE ♦ /

This area, lift, and run which appeared in 1999 were named by Tim Blixseth, the developer of the condos at the base of the lift. Moose, an Algonquian Indian name meaning "twig eater," frequent the

Moose   *Mike Lockhart*

38

willows by this stream, and thus the name.

There is a famous quote from the 1909 *Ballads of a Cheechako* by Robert W. Service:

Follow and follow a lone moose trail, till you come to a valley grim,
On the slope of the lonely watershed that borders the Polar brim.

Hardly grim or Arctic, the lower elevation and location make this a good place to go on cold, windy days. The run follows the lift with interesting bumps and a complex fall line.

LONE PEAK TRIPLE/ AND TRAM/

Rising to 11,166 feet, this mountain is the signature of Big Sky/Moonlight Basin. Its lone position is due to the fact that it was formed by a magma intrusion that resisted the glaciers that removed the surrounding sedimentary rock.

The Triple chair was present at the opening of the resort with the first black diamond in the Bowl. When the Tram went to the top in 1995, the mountain achieved the status of one of the great ski areas in the world.

LONE WOLF ●

The green "wolf" run to go with blue Lobo and the black Mad Wolf, this nice mellow run goes under the Explorer chair to Chet's Knob. Easy hills and flats make this a perfect learner's run.

Lone Wolf, Gul-pa-Go, was a Kiowa chief who lived from 1820 to 1879. In his lawsuit, Lone Wolf v. Hitchcock, the Supreme Court ruled that Indians were wards of the state, like criminals and mentally insane, and as such did not have the same Constitutional human rights as full citizens. They further ruled that Congress had the power to change treaty terms without consent. The ruling still stands and its principles continue to influence the relationship to Native American tribes today.

Lone Wolf

LOW BENCH ◆

This is an area below the rock band on the right side of the Bowl at the start of the Turkey Traverse. It is a good area to look for a powder line after the Bowl has been tracked. See *Mary's Bush* which is located here.

In geology, a bench is a long, relatively narrow strip of level or gently inclined land that is bounded by distinctly steeper slopes above and below.

LOW CLEARING ◆

At the bottom right of the Highway just before entering Lower Morningstar, this steep open area can have nice moguls and snow. Being south facing, it can also be icy and firm in the morning.

LOW DOG ♦

Named for the road that it parallels, this track is the exit from War Dance, Marlboro Country, and the Mine Shaft back to the Thunderwolf lift.

All of the original roads in Big Sky were named for actual Native Americans. Low Dog was born in 1846 and was one of the fighting chiefs of the Oglala Sioux at the Little Big Horn where Custer was killed. To the Indians, he was known as "a wild, daring devil," and one particular story tells of how he wounded a mail carrier near Wolf Point, MT, pegged him to the ground, piled grass around him, and set it afire. Enjoy the run, but don't emulate his behavior.

Low Dog

Wolf   *Gary Kramer*

MAD WOLF ♦

The historic Mad Wolf was a Blackfoot chief whose name in that language was Sai-yeh. He is commemorated with Mount Siyeh, in Glacier National Park, one of six peaks over 10,000 feet in the park. It is easily seen and reached on a hike from Siyeh Bend on Going-to-the Sun road.

The primary black diamond run on Andesite, it is known for its long stretch of moguls. Entry can be from directly over the cornice for a steep, short drop, or more easily by staying near the trees that border the right and left sides. Following the headwall, skiers can continue down the bumps or drop into the easier valley of Madison Avenue. The traverse across to Elk Park to meet your spouse makes a nice exit and will allow you to wander the powder of Elk Park Meadows.

MADISON AVENUE ■

This run is a groomed strip to the left on Mad Wolf that is entered from the upper right of Elk Park Ridge. It can also serve as an escape for your knees that have had enough of the demanding black diamond bumps of Mad Wolf.

Although Lone Peak in is Madison County, from the river that Lewis and Clark named for James Madison, our fourth president; this run's name comes from the street in New York City. Carrying through with the "Mad" theme, this is wide and stately like the avenue. There are perhaps a few less people here than in Manhattan, and the hotel prices are much cheaper.

MAGIC MEADOWS ♦

Turn after the blue square #12 sign on the tree on BRT Traverse and follow any of a number of tight lines through the trees that come out on Lower Morningstar. Going farther along BRT Traverse to where it takes the big left turn leads to the variation of the Magic Meadows that locals call "Challenger Trees". Going straight into the trees instead of taking the left turn takes you to this line of small meadows and trees that parallels the lift. It comes out on the Challenger Lift Line near the base of the Challenger lift.

Magic Meadows is an area that skiers and boarders found for the fun of it. It became so popular that the resort put a name on it.

By the way, the blue square #12 sign has nothing to do with Magic Meadows, which is a true black diamond tree run that intermediates should avoid. The sign just says that you are on BRT Traverse (#12 on some of the old trail maps), but it makes a good clue on where to enter the Magic Meadows.

MAGNUM COULOIR ●

A bit tongue in cheek, this flat track was cut to provide access from Lower Morningstar to White Wing, the Beaverhead condos, and the First Aid room.

MARLBORO COUNTRY ♦ ♦

The fences on War Dance are used to control slides and were placed on the rock face that does not hold snow well. Following the fence line to the right through the trees gets to Peru, a small meadow on the continuation of this rock face. You will now be in Marlboro Country. To help you find it, a roped gate has been placed at the entry for the 2010-11 season.

This is rocky, rough and tumble stuff, so you have to be one tough cowboy to ski Marlboro Country.

In 1960 Phillip Morris created Marlboro Country to market their cigarette with a the image of a rugged cowboys. "Come to where the flavor is... come to MARLBORO COUNTRY", backed by Elmer Bernstein's theme from The Magnificent Seven. The first Marlboro man was a rancher from near Wolf Creek, Montana and was known to the author. He died of lung cancer.

Marmot   *Inklein*

MARMOT MEADOWS ■

This short run of a blue square returns to the base area near the bottom of Mr. K by cutting over to the run-out to Crazy Horse. The right turn at the top of the last big hill on Mr K is well signed. It has a moderate pitch and a couple moguls for practice before you try the bigger stuff.

The Yellow-bellied Marmot, *Marmota flaviventris*, is common in the Big Sky area. A hibernator, you will not see him during ski season. Weighing 5-11 lbs this relative to the squirrel and woodchuck lives in rock piles and can be heard whistling when danger or humans approach. Our sister ski area near Vancouver, B.C. is named for his bigger cousin, the Whistler or Hoary Marmot, *Marmota caligata*.

MARX ♦♦

Along with Lenin, this is one of the signature runs off the Tram. Steep and open, at the end of the Yeti Traverse, it often collects deep snow that blows over from Liberty Bowl. This beautiful, open bowl is a joy to ski in itself, but Marx also leads to the Gullies Traverse, Tohelluride, and the Dirtbag Wall. The exit is on the Duck Walk for a return lap, or continue straight over the Duck Walk down Yellow Mule for a continuous 2700' vertical feet of black diamond. Are your legs still there?

Karl Marx

Named by skiers when this was a hiking area before the Tram, the resort tried to rename Marx and Lenin as Thunder and Lightning. Tradition held, and Marx is what it has remained. Communists and really bad dudes notwithstanding, this can be a sweet run on a bluebird day in the powder.

MARY'S BUSH ♦

Just below the Low Bench in the Bowl, skier's right, is a solitary tree that in deep snow looks like a bush. Good powder lines are available by cutting under the Low Bench rocks to this bush.

It is named for Mary, a volunteer ski patroller, who was on the Jay Walk and called the patrol for a person down and not moving in the Bowl. The "person" turned out to be this bush.

MIDDLE RIDER ●

Serving as a feeder to the homes on Middle Rider Road, the name comes from the road. This is a popular surname among the Blackfeet. The Middle Rider family is documented back as far as 1800 and has included many medicine men, chiefs, and warriors.

MIDDLE ROAD ■

This is a service road that goes from Liberty Bowl and the Shedhorn area to become the run-out road for Chuck's, Stump Farm, Lobo and Calamity Jane back to the base area. It goes around the middle of the mountain, as opposed to the higher Duck Walk, but can be very slow going.

When the Shedhorn lift is down, it is the only return from Liberty Bowl. One must take care to stay high on the shoulder bottom left of Screaming Left to catch the traverse to the road. Too low and into Sunlight takes one below the road for a long hike back up.

The run to the base via Liberty Bowl and Middle Road is the longest on the mountain - 6 miles.

MIDNIGHT ♦

Paralleling left of Moonlight off the top of the Challenger, this run has some nice little meadows and trees that hold snow well. As the meadow closes in, skiers and riders can return right to Moonlight, or continue straight down the tight steep Midnight Trees to the Fast Lane.

The name was just an apt partner to Moonlight.

MINE SHAFT ♦

Staying skier's left on War Dance, or coming off the bottom of Colter's Hell to the right takes you down a steep narrow shaft through some young lodgepole pine. The run out along Low Dog gets you back to the Thunderwolf lift.

The name, duh! Mine shafts are neither flat nor wide.

MOONLIGHT ♦

The "easy" route off Challenger, this wide open run goes left of the lift and on down to the Fast Lane. Well travelled, it picks up some large, but rhythmic moguls. Like our coyotes, it is OK to howl with joy to the moonlight as you go down this run.

The name comes from Moonlight Meadows, a name given to a set of aspen groves and clearings that was the site of a hunting camp years ago. The name was adopted by one of the signature resorts of this area, Moonlight Basin, but the run came well before the formation of this resort.

A warning: Moonlight is five times brighter at this altitude than at sea level, intensifying its stimulation to romance.

MOOSE TRACKS (snowshoe)

This snowshoe and hiking trail from the top of the Swiftcurrent lift to the base was named for our moose. *Alces alces,* the largest member of the deer family that is common in the Big Sky area. "Moose" comes from an Algonquian Indian word meaning "twig eater" with a preferred food of willow and aspen. Local homeowners can find them munching on the landscape shrubbery in their yards throughout the winter.

MORA'S ♦

This short run from the Jay Walk is between Great White and the Gondola Shaft and gets you to the cat track to Rice Bowl.

It was named for Mora Longdon, a patroller who caught a tree here and injured her ACL.

MORNING STAR ● ■

Highest run outside the Bowl in original plan, this is the longest run of a single name on the mountain. A blue square as Upper Morning Star off the Triple chair, it continues to the base area as the green dot of Lower Morning Star.

Upper Morningstar goes past the Tram house, either left or right - watch out for the gully - then follows the open ridge. A sweeping right turn near the end avoids the black diamond Gun Mount and takes you to the Triple chair, either via

Little Coyote and Morning Star   Edward S. Curtis

the cat track to the right or through the mogul field straight ahead. It is an easy run that is only difficult, due to the lack of features, in a whiteout cloud. Upper Morningstar is good for the intermediates in the group when others, braver or crazier, want to do the Bowl.

Lower Morningstar starts off the Jay Walk and takes the cat track to the left of the start of Mr K. Long, wide and easy, it parallels Mr K to the base, or goes to the Explorer lift via White Wing. This is a great beginner's practice slope.

Although the morning star is the name given to the planet Venus when it appears in the East before sunrise, this run was named by Chet Huntley. His interest in Native American names means that it commemorates Motaĺake 'hnĺxahpo, Morning Star, a chief of the Cheyenne. Known as Dull Knife by the whites, this is an English translation of the name given him by his allies the Sioux. The Dull Knife fight that occurred after the Battle of the Little Bighorn resulted in the destruction of 153 lodges and many war ponies, and led to the Cheyenne surrender and transportation to Oklahoma. Faced with disease and starvation, Morning Star and Little Coyote led the escape back to Montana and Morning Star and a large number of the tribe were killed by the US Army in Nebraska. Little Coyote and the few survivors made it to SE Montana where they were allowed to remain. Chief Dull Knife College in Lame Deer, Montana was named in his honor.

MR K ●

This greatest of the green runs drops 1750 feet over nearly 3 miles. Take the Jay Walk from the top of Swiftcurrent lift, and you will find Mr. K starting directly behind the loading area for the Triple Chair. With a few easy hills and long steady flats, it is a great run for the beginning skier to practice technique, or just to enjoy the long steady joy of skiing.

Originally this run was called Killifer after Tom Killifer, CFO of Chrysler,

Everett Kircher   Boyne Resorts archives

44

and one of the original board members of the group that started Big Sky. With the purchase of the resort in 1976 by Boyne USA it was renamed Mr. K in honor of Everett Kircher. Mr. Kircher founded the business that became Boyne USA in 1947. Under his leadership it became the country's largest private group of ski resorts, and developed into an all season operation with golf courses, hotels and cross country ski areas as well. Not only a resort businessman, he also patented equipment for snow making, introduced new methods of ski instruction, and was innovative in the use of new chairlifts. Where Chet Huntley was the inspiration that formed Big Sky, Everett Kircher was the force that made it great. He died at the age of 85 in 2002, and his family continues his tradition.

MULE SKINNER ♦

A feeder trail from the Shedhorn to the Dakota lifts can be found by heading above Sunrise to the sign at the bottom of Screaming Left. You wonder why a connecter cat track is a black diamond? A mule skinner in the slang vernacular is someone who drives mules. This is done by laying a healthy lash or whip to their backs. After you've been over the rocks, trees and stumps on this trail, you'll feel like the mule.

A better route to the Dakota Territory is down from Liberty Bowl.

NAMELESS TRAIL ●

Kids named and made these series of winding trails off to the side of Mr K. With branches designed for short persons, this run gives the kids their first taste of glades.

NATURAL HALF PIPE●

This fun little gully can be entered from the top left of Mr. K or on the right near the top of Lower Morning Star. It is indeed a naturally formed half pipe. Good for practicing your moves, Dude!

Heading straight at the bottom, instead of the left to Lower Morning Star, leads into the trees for a little glade skiing favored by the local kids.

NEVER SWEAT ♦a

This run starts towards the Tram house from the top of the Triple. Stay hard right around the *Forested Knoll* and you will find a natural curved half pipe that bends around the Knoll, under the Triple chair, and out into the Bowl. The steep walls and complex fall line make for an interesting run. It is short, and none of the steeps go very far, so you "never sweat" if you fall.

This is a great place to practice self-arrest. It is steep enough for your body to slide, but poor technique is not punished, as the hike back up to your skis is short.

NOSE ♦ a

Also called *Booger Nugget,* this short, steep drop off the north end of the *Forested Knoll* goes into the bottom of Never Sweat.

Not clear whether this is a Roman or button, it is not a Bob Hope ski jump; so don't blow it!

O GULLY a

This is the ski patrol name for the avalanche chute or path just below the Buttress that leads to the Gun Mount area.

OLD TIPPY'S ■

When the Summit Hotel was built in 2000, Tippy's Tumble as a groomer had to be rerouted. The previous route was left as an ungroomed mogul run with an obvious entrance off to the right on Tippy's just above the final headwall.

It is a good place to practice mogul and powder technique as it is rather short. You can also show off for the four-star guests watching from the Summit windows. Have fun where Tippy Huntley took her tumble

ONSLOW'S ♦ ♦

Terry Onslow was the ski patrol director from 1977-79. This steep tight double black route is between Little Tree and the Zucchini Patch off the bottom of Country Club on the Little Rock Tongue.

River otter
Rocky Mountain National Park

OTTER SLIDE ♦ ♦

This is an extremely steep entrance to Marx and Lenin that leaves directly from the upper Tram house. An easier and safer approach starts down Liberty Bowl with a left onto the Yeti Traverse.

Both Otter and Yeti, the two routes to Marx and Lenin from the top, were German shepherd ski patrol dogs who graciously gave their names to these runs.

The North American River otter *Lontra canadensis* is known for its playful behavior. One such is a belly slide down mud or snow into the river. Some true otter slides have been reported to be several hundred yards long. Be careful up here that you do not mimic this playful mustilid!

OUTER LIMITS ♦ ♦

The open rocky talus field farthest left off the top of Challenger and Midnight goes down into the trees and is called the Outer Limits for its location, farthest from the lift. Locals tend to call the tree section straight ahead "Midnight Trees" and the "Cliff", so marked by the "Danger Cliff!" sign for the area in the trees to the left. Which brings to mind the question, Why put the danger sign here when you are already committed?

The Outer Limits was an early sci-fi TV mystery. Each show would begin with a narration by someone identifying himself as the Control Voice:

> *"There is nothing wrong with your television set. Do not attempt to adjust the picture. We are controlling transmission. If we wish to make it louder, we will bring up the volume. If we wish to make it softer, we will tune it to a whisper.... For the next hour, sit quietly and we will control all that you see and hear. We repeat: there is nothing wrong with your television set. You are about to participate in a great adventure. You are about to experience the awe and mystery which reaches from the inner mind to... The Outer Limits. "*

PACKSADDLE GLADES ♦

Between Dude Park and Paradise from the Duck Walk or Middle Road, this run through the trees parallels Dude Park to Cow Flats for the return to the Shedhorn lift. It takes a bit of effort to get to this run, so it is a good place to find a powder stash late in the day.

In line with the Shedhorn area's backcountry horse theme, this name fits with Yellow Mule and Mule Skinner. A packsaddle is used to carry gear, and lends its name to pack horse, pack trip, and pack train. The most familiar type is the wooden sawbuck. The cross trees on this saddle are appropriate reminders for the terrain in this glade.

PACIFIER ●

When the green dot runs on Southern Comfort were constructed, an easy return was necessary to get back down the Rancharger side of Andesite. The old service road and trail to Africa was widened and smoothed. It is now the preferred beginner's route. It starts just below the Ramcharger lift and traverses to the left over the top of Hangman's and Africa to a big hairpin turn to return to the base by passing under Africa, Safari, and Hangman's. A little attention to the less skilled exiting these runs above you would be prudent.

An artificial nipple that is used to sooth and comfort infants, the name is appropriate for an inexperienced skier facing this or Ambush to get home. In other English speaking countries, this device is also called a "dummy" but we won't get into that.

PARACHUTE ♦ ♦

One of the A-Z Chutes, this is the widest, and from below has the biggest saddle. The name is obvious. Bring your helmet, transceiver, probe, shovel, and rip cord.

PARADISE ♦

The farthest glade run along the Duck Walk before coming to the Swiftcurrent lift, Paradise can also be entered from the top of Swifty by traversing high across Lobo Meadows and going through the orange roped gate in the trees. Steep, and often full of great snow, it drops down a wide meadow into some huge, widely spaced conifers.

After coming out on a short, flat run-out, you will have a choice of a long, flat Middle Road trip to the base area, or a long, flat trip down Cow Flats to Shedhorn. Hey, that was Paradise! No one promised you that after all that glory life would be easy.

PARKIN'S PARADISE ♦

Between Arch and Stutzman's Rocks on the South Wall, the line was named for this patroller. Like all of the South Wall, some sweet powder can be found here.

PERU ♦♦

Officially opened with a gate for the first time for the 2010-11 season, this glade to the skier's right of War Dance and beyond Bolivia, was named for its shape, like that of the country. It is in Marlboro Country and comes out on Low Dog. Tight and gnarly, it is best left to the llamas.

PINNACLES ♦

Across the top of Country Club to the big tree is a traverse that leads to this run. It is really the northern most extension of the A-Z Chute country and is named for the tall, yellow limestone rocks that you ski around. There are several routes down through these rocks. One is called "Once is Enough" because it requires a hard left turn out of a narrow chute, or you go off a 60' cliff.

A pinnacle, from Latin pinnaculum, a little feather, is an architectural ornament. The pinnacle looks like a small spire and was mainly used in Gothic architecture. The word has since been expanded to refer to geologic structures such as mountains and rock towers that resemble the architectural spire.

PONDEROSA ■

The easiest of Big Sky's blue runs goes straight off the Ramcharger lift and down to the Southern Comfort. Getting to it from the Southern Comfort lift requires a right turn to follow the cat track and turning right when you can. The run has a few little hills to negotiate, but is considerably less steep than Calamity, Lobo, or the blues on the Ramcharger side - a good introduction.

Pinus ponderosa, the Ponderosa or Yellow Pine, is one of the dominant evergreen species in the West. It is a long needled pine and uncommon in the drier, east slope around Big Sky. It carries a real Western flavor because of the Ponderosa Ranch from the TV series Bonanza. The ghostly images of Adam, Ben, Hoss, and Little Joe have been reported on this trail.

POWDER RIVER ■

In extreme southeastern Montana, Powder River county, with Broadus the county seat, has a huge population of 1850 souls. It is name comes from the Powder River that flows north through here to join the Yellowstone some 50 miles south of Miles City. Some feel that the river was named for its naturally muddy condition that settlers said was "too thin to plow and too thick to drink", but it was actually named by Wm Clark for the sand along the banks that resembled gunpowder. The lonely upper reaches are the site of the Hole-in-the-Wall hideout of Butch Cassidy and the Sundance Kid's Wild Bunch Gang, and the geologic oddity, Hell's Half Acre. The Powder River Basin is now a major source of low-sulfur coal.

Gentle and ambling, except for the first waterfall that could be called Hell's Half Acre, this Ironhorse run resembles the river.

RAINBOW ROCK ♦

Between Black Rock and Arch Rock on the South Wall, this line was named for the colorful rock in the band above the Turkey Traverse that marks it.

RAMCHARGER /

When the old and slow original Ram's Horn lift was replaced in 1990, a charged up name was necessary for this first high speed quad. Chrysler Corporation was contacted for permission to use the name of their big truck, which was all the more appropriate as Chrysler was one of the original founding partners in Chet Huntley's Big Sky.

Ramshorn Mountain is the triangular peak east on the Gallatin range, visible from the top of Bighorn and as you drive down the Spur Road. At 10,289' it is the highest point on that range.

Ram's Horn Lift early days   Boyne USA

RAMP SHOT a

This is an avalanche control site that is located just above the exit ramp to the Triple Chair. It is carefully controlled particularly because of the heavy use, but it is also evidence that some seemingly mild slopes can be dangerous. This slope, because of its position, gets wind loaded with snow.

RAT HOLE'S REVENGE ♦ ♦ a

This is the nickname of the original head of the ski patrol, Jim Kanssler, and designates that open area on the bottom left of the First Gully above the top of the Triple chair's lift and patrol shack. It is important for avalanche control to keep the entrance to The Bowl and Turkey Traverse safe. Looking up to the right from the chair, the remains of an old rope tow can be seen. This was used before the Tram to get patrollers up to plant charges on this area and above The Bowl.

RAY'S RIDGE ♦

Coming down off the right of the run Moonlight is a talus field that turns into a ridge one can follow into the trees. Left out of the trees brings you back to Moonlight, and a right turn drops down into BRT North. The run was named for Ray Tout, an engineer for Chrysler, whose realty branch was one of the prime investors in Chet Huntley's original Big Sky development consortium. Ray was the only member of the original Big Sky group who stayed into the Boyne management times. Ray and his wife, Margaret, lived in Big Sky until his death about 10 yrs ago. He is credited with the surveying for the original lifts and much of the infrastructure at the resort.

RICE BOWL ♦

When Gondola I was running, a road went from the lift house to Calamity Jane and Lobo along the top of The Rice Bowl. The road still exists and can be reached by taking a hard right off the Jay Walk above the Triple Chair, dropping down Great White or its cousins, or by going left off Calamity Jane under the Swiftcurrent Chair. Anywhere below the road are good lines through the trees and the dead pines that were killed by beetles in the 1970s. Powder tends to be the best of all the runs off Swifty and the exit is into Crazy Horse to return to the base. A locals' hidden traverse to the right through the trees at the bottom of Rice Bowl leads to Buffalo Jump and a bit more steep before the return.

In addition to the shape, and being a small bowl, the Rice Bowl was also named for the granular snow and depth hoar that forms there.

RIFFLE ■

This short bit of moguls was cut off Powder River to give a bit more interest on the blue Iron Horse runs. It drops to the right under the lift and across the cat track to Moonlight Lodge, before entering the run-out of Bad Dog back to the lift.

A riffle is a shallow stretch of a river or stream, where the swifter current forms small rippled waves. It is probably a good name for this portion of an otherwise Class I run.

RISING BULL ●

An access trail to a subdivision, this is another of the runs named for the street. As with most of the early streets, this one also was named for an historic Native American. Rising Bull was chief of the Blackfoot from about 1840 until his death in the measles winter of 1859-60. He was also known as the chief of two tribes since he married a Flathead woman and was a chief with her tribe before moving back over the divide to return to the Blackfoot. Rising Bull Ridge, formerly Mt Rockwell, between Lone Walker and Sinopah Mountains, on the south side of Upper Two Medicine Lake in Glacier Park, is named for him.

ROCK POCKET ♦ ♦

This is a favorite special place because of the consistently good snow and rhythmic moguls. Originally the bottom end of the Snake Pit, the better entrance is through a gate at the bottom right of Broken Arrow just below where this run joins Mad Wolf. The name is apparent from the cliff and rocky jumble to your right as you enter the run. After turning left below the rocks, this run turns into a moderately wide, straight, steep mogul field that empties into the lower flats of Bighorn.

The lower section is also known as *"Everett's Anger"* for Everett Kircher's opinion when he found out that his son John had cut this run. Thanks, John!

In spite of the fact that David Stutzman was killed in an avalanche here in

1983 (See Stutzman's Rock), this is not a particularly dangerous area. Care and a transceiver are always indicated in steep areas with loose snow.

ROCKVILLE BOWL ♦♦

Lying below the Vuarnet Cliffs and The Wave, a whole pile of big rocks have fallen off these cliffs and clustered here - thus the name.

Short, but with great snow and pitch, this bowl is entered by cutting below the cliffs from Castro, or by dropping down off the Wave's cornice. Skiing into it over the Vuarnet Cliffs requires a rope and belay or zero brains.

ROSEBUD ●

The housing access trail from Rosebud Street to the White Otter lift was not named for the dying words of Orson Wells' character in the movie Citizen Kane.

This name follows the Big Sky penchant for Native American names. The Battle of the Rosebud occurred June 17, 1876 during the Black Hills War. In the battle, Crazy Horse and his Cheyenne allies halted the advance of General Crook and forced him to return to his base camp at Goose Creek. This prevented him from joining up with the 7th Cavalry under George Armstrong Custer before the Battle of the Little Bighorn, and gave great inspiration to the Indians. The battle site is preserved at the Rosebud Battlefield State Park in Big Horn County, Montana.

SACAJAWEA ●

Unquestionably the most famous Native American woman in American history, Sacajawea (c. 1788-1812) was a Shoshone woman who accompanied the Lewis and Clark Expedition, acting as an interpreter and guide. Although reliable historical information about Sacagawea is very limited, she has become an important part of the Lewis and Clark mythology.

Starting with a left turn as one gets off the Southern Comfort lift, this runs a bit with Deep South before turning downhill. Smooth and rolling, it rejoins Deep South for the run-out back to the lift. Watch out for the roped off ice from the spring on the run-out.

Be like this famous Indian woman and explore this lovely green slope, showing the men how to do it.

SADDLE RIDGE ●

A saddle ridge is named for the familiar concave shape of a horse's saddle. Seen as a low slope along a ridge it is the usual route of a crossing trail. This is the access cat track to the Saddle Ridge condos and Moonlight Lodge.

SAFARI ●

Entering from the upper left of Hangman's, a name was needed for the easiest route that goes over the top of Congo and into Africa. Why not a safari?

Well groomed and of a mellow pitch, this run allows skiers to try a few moguls on Africa, and then retreat to the groomed when it gets too gnarly. As it turns back to the base area, it passes under the exit to the Congo. Stop off to the side and look up to watch people dance down through the trees of this glade.

St Alphonse di Liguori

ST ALPHONSE TREES ♦

Where 17 Green and Highway separate is a cluster of trees that parallels the left side of the Highway back to BRT Traverse. This is St Alphonse's glade and can be a nice tight trip in good snow. Continuing from St Alphonse straight across BRT Traverse leads into the Magic Meadows and on to Lower Morningstar.

Alphonsus Mary Antony John Cosmas Damian Michael Gaspard de' Liguori (1696-1787) was a Neapolitan Catholic bishop, spiritual writer, theologian, and founder of the Redemptorists religious order. He was canonized in 1839. Pray to St Alphonse all ye who enter here!

SECRET ENTRANCE ♦ ♦

This cutoff from the bottom of the Big Couloir into the Little Couloir is quite rocky in usual seasons. On the other hand, if you have done "The Big" you can probably sneak over here successfully.

Sshhhh! It's a secret.

SCREAMING LEFT ♦

The bottom of Liberty Bowl enters a natural half pipe valley that takes a sharp left turn before exiting onto Sunlight. Staying up along the top right ridge avoids the valley and allows a few steep turns down the moguls before the blue of Sunlight. The valley bottom is a nice easy route for legs pooped by Liberty, or ride the pipe for an alternating fall line.

The name came from the early days of the Tram when a downhill race course was contemplated for Liberty Bowl. With the speed generated down this steep run, a "screaming left" turn would be necessary to avoid hurtling off into the trees.

SHADY CHUTE ♦ ♦

Entering the trees to the left of Elk Park Ridge will get you into Marlboro Country. Along the skier's right of Marlboro Country is a glade section pioneered by Bob Dixon and Rick Davis. It is tight and difficult and exits onto Low Dog.

SHEDHORN /

This lift, installed 1995, was named for Shedhorn Mountain at 9987' and the creek of the same name that are located a few miles south in the Lee Metcalf Wilderness between Big Sky and the Taylor Fork

Christmas of 1996 saw a huge snowfall, and avalanche control was suspended because of the tragic death of patroller Erica Pankow. (see Erica's Glade) The following day, the snow load generated a massive avalanche down Lenin that tore out the upper Shedhorn lift and patrol house, as well as several towers. Fortunately, no one was there at the time, so no one was hurt, but skiing Shedhorn was done for the season. The towers were reinstalled, the house replaced with a concrete bunker, and a berm built at the bottom of Lenin to help deflect future slides. As you ride up the Shedhorn lift, look to your right and a few hundred yards below the top you will see an orange ski patrol sled high in a pine tree. This is a remnant and reminder of that giant slide.

SHORT SHOT ♦ ♦ a

This is the open area on the bottom of the First Gully and next to the Rat Hole's Revenge. It frequently needs avalanche control to keep the Turkey Traverse and the entrance to The Bowl open and safe, and is a "short shot" from the Avalauncher.

SHOSHONE CONDOMINIUM HOTEL

This modern addition to the Huntley Lodge was opened 1990. The Shoshone, or Snake Indian, Tribe were the primary Native American residents in the Big Sky area. Their reservations are currently in Idaho and Utah. The most famous Shoshone was Sacagawea, the only woman on the Lewis and Clark Corps of Discovery. She has been commemorated in the Sacajawea Dollar and on our run on Southern Comfort.

SILVER KNIFE ■

One of the original blue runs at Big Sky, this sets a nice pitch to practice your turns. Being the farthest groomer on skier's right of the Ramcharger lift, it can hold fresh tracks in new snow longer than Ambush or Tippy's. This run is also the preferred way to the Arrowhead building. Stop at the ski rack on the run-out for a good lunch at The Cabin, a brew at Scissorbill's, or a visit to Lone Mountain Sports.

Tosawi or Silver Knife was a Penateka Comanche chief deemed "cooperative" by the US Army. He is best known for an alleged exchange with Gen. Philip Sheridan where Sheridan purportedly stated "The only good Indian is a dead Indian". Sheridan denied making that statement.

Tosawi 1872

SLOT ♦

This is the unofficial name that locals have given the most leftward line on the Bowl. Directly under the Triple chair and with the Forested Knoll to the immediate left, it is the steepest route down until the South Wall

SNAKE BITE ♦

A bar drink of half and half Stout Beer and Hard Cider, it can also be made with Jack Daniel's, Tequila and Tabasco; or Vodka, Green Chartreuse and Tabasco. Whatever the recipe, this run can make you feel like you have had (or need) several.

This is the farthest west of the Big Sky runs, and comes off the cat track to your right as you leave the Iron Horse lift. Go too far on this track and you will be on Elkhorn and into Moonlight Basin. If you do Snake Bite, be sure to take the first right back onto Powder River. The natural exit is to Cinnabar, and once again you will be in Moonlight, and will have some difficulty getting back to the Big Sky side. Steep, a bit winding like a snake, it is full of moguls. This run can be infested with the legendary snow snakes, imaginary critters that cause inexplicable falls.

SNAKE PIT ♦ ♦

This tight tree run is the most difficult named glade on the Andesite trail map. With an access gate on Bighorn just above and running parallel to Bear Lair, it, too, is famous for its snow snakes.

Although when this trail was logged, a den of snakes was reputed to have been uncovered here, this is not the derivation of the name. The Ski Patrollers say that the name comes because it is a very dangerous area where the avalanches funnel down into a terrain trap. In either case, the name fits this steep, tight, difficult glade.

SNOWCREST LODGE

Opened in 1998, this building houses lockers, restrooms, ski school, ticketing, and, on the third floor, private slopeside condominiums. The name is purely fanciful.

SOUTH FACE

The South Wall faces north, but, the South Face is an area looking south. It is the open part of the Peak where you can find Dakota Territory, Liberty Bowl, Marx, Lenin, and their kin.

SOUTH GLADES ■

The regular return to Thunderwolf from the Lone Moose lift is the Wapiti, a cat track off Little Dogie. Being very flat, people began cutting through the trees for this return, and this route was eventually opened as an official run. As you start away from the top of the lift, look right and you will see the entrance. The glades face south and give a couple of turns past widely spaced trees back to the right side of Bighorn. On a powder day, good snow can be had by coming out of this glade with a zig-zag traverse and staying up in the little trees high on the right side of Bighorn.

SOUTH WALL ♦

Out near the end of the Turkey Traverse, this widest steep section is a good warm up for your Tram run. Facing North, it is cold and shaded in the early season, but, because of this, often keeps excellent snow.

From the Low Bench rocks to Black Rock are several avalanche paths named for the rocks above: Jefferson, Madison, Gallatin, and Yellowstone (with yellow lichen) from west to east. The rocks are covered in big snow years, and the names are not runs, but used by the avalanche patrollers to designate slide routes to control.

SOUTHERN COMFORT /

Installed in 1990 and upgraded to a high speed quad chair in 2005, these runs were designed for the resort's southern visitors. Groups from Florida, Alabama, and Georgia have been longstanding clientele and love these warm, gentle south facing slopes.

STUMP FARM ♦

Going straight off Lobo Meadows after the valley, and before it turns left to return to main Lobo, leads to the Stump Farm. Self explanatory in the early days, the stumps have since been cleared, but the run remains a challenge. A large rock cliff with a huge fumarole in the middle of the run gives two routes around it, left and right. Both have complex fall lines and, because they are narrow, tend to get scraped off during times of low snow adding further to the challenge.

STUTZMAN'S ROCK ♦

This rock on the South Wall, and labeled on the trail map, was named for David Stutzman who, in a whiteout, unknowingly skied over it, suffering some significant discomfort.

Stutzman was an accomplished mountaineer who in 1982 had made a first ascent in the Himalayas. Shortly after his return to Big Sky, on Christmas Eve day, he was buried in an avalanche in the Rock Pocket and died. The rock was named in his honor.

SUMMIT HOTEL

The Summit Hotel opened Mar 2000 as the European style luxury residence at Big Sky. Although clearly not at the 11.144' summit, this is the four star peak of luxury at Big Sky.

SUMMIT SNOWFIELD a

Not to be confused with the North Summit Snowfield that is a Moonlight Basin area off the summit, this is purely an avalanche path. It lies under the Tram between the Big Couloir and the Chamber Pot.

SUNLIGHT ■

This is the only blue run and the only groomed run on Shedhorn. It can be found going farthest skier's right from the lift, or as the collector for skiers coming off Liberty Bowl.

Many of the runs off the Shedhorn lift were named for local geographic landmarks. This is no exception. A hike up Wapiti Creek, with a trailhead up the Taylor Fork road 15 miles south of Big Sky brings you to Sunlight Basin. It is directly east and 1000' below Pika Point, both popular summer hiking destinations.

Sunlight, solar radiation from the sun, is responsible for life on earth. What a great life cruising down this mellow blue run on Shedhorn.

SURE SHOT ♦ ♦ a

This avalanche path is at the top of the Bowl just after the entrance. It is quite skiable from 1st Gully and gets its name from the fact that it is low and close to the Avalauncher, making it a "sure shot".

SWIFT CURRENT /

Called "Swifty" by the locals, this high speed quad chairlift was installed in 1996. It originally just replaced Gondola I, but now both gondolas have been retired for age and safety reasons.

The lift's name, in addition to the reference to the speed of the high speed quad, is a tribute to the beautiful Swiftcurrent area in the Many Glacier Valley of Glacier National Park. The Swiftcurrent Glacier is near the pass of the same name and on the east side of the Garden Wall of the Continental Divide.

SWIFTY LIFT LINE ♦

The Swiftcurrent lift line can be followed from the top, but the section just below the entrance to the Buffalo Jump gets quite black diamond gnarly. For a better route, get a little speed off the bottom of the Calamity Jane headwall and take a slight angle left up to the top of the hill and the start of the mellow, blue square part of this run.

A terrain park has been established here. It should be noted that the larger individuals you can observe are parents who are rarely seen on the features, and then only by mistake or poor judgment. It is a great place for the lift riders to be impressed as the young, flexible bodies either score or crash and burn.

TANGO TREES ♦

This is a short run through the trees is at the top left of Crazy Horse. You can dance through this, wiggling your butt in good Latin American style.

THE TRAM/

See Lone Peak Tram.

THREE FORKS ■

The unofficial name given to the wide run off the end of the Andesite cat track that serves as access to Elk Park Ridge, Tippy's Tumble, and Silver Knife. Ignoring War Dance and the various glades, you can see why it is called "Three" Forks. Three Forks, MT is a small town population 1800 some 25 miles east of Bozeman off I-90. It was named for the Three Forks of the Missouri that signify the start of that great river. Named by Lewis and Clark, the Gallatin, Madison, and Jefferson Rivers come together here at the Headwaters State Park.

THUNDERWOLF/

Originally a slow double chair, the Mad Wolf lift installed in 1979 opened the north east side of Andesite. It was replaced in 1994 with a high speed quad that was renamed Thunderwolf for speed.

TIPPY'S TUMBLE ■

Found by staying on left side of *Three Forks* off the Andesite cat track, Tippy's is smooth, wide and straight with a bit of a pitch. It is one of the sweet blues on Andesite and has been homologated by the FIS for slalom and GS racing.

It was named for Tippy Stringer Huntley, Chet's second wife. She had been the "Weather Girl" on WRC-TV in Washington D.C. where the NBC Nightly News originated, and they were married in 1959. After Chet Huntley's death in 1973, she made a brief unsuccessful bid for the Senate seat from Montana. Tippy left the area shortly thereafter and married William Conrad, star of the "Cannon" TV detective series.

TITS UP a

Charlie Pearson, a patroller working the cornice above the Gullies, triggered an avalanche and surfed a chunk of snow on his back down into the Bowl. A scary ride, but he survived after "a ton" of stitches. His "tits were up" and the name is now used for this avalanche path.

TODD'S HOLE ♦ ♦

This steep route goes through the trees off the middle right of Moonlight. It follows Moonlight down the last headwall for some good, steep powder. It was named for Todd Pritcher, an early ski patroller.

TOHELLURIDE ♦ ♦

This wall, to the left on Marx, was named by John Kircher. Some nice lines are available, particularly with good powder, but it is a tricky, rocky slope that can be Hell.

Punned, but not named after a ski area next to the town of Telluride, CO, Telluride resort has a total of 120 runs and 2,000+ acres of skiable terrain and a 3845' lift served vertical drop. A world class resort, it has hardly the class of Big Sky or this run. Telluride is an mineral anion of Tellurium, an element used in alloys and a byproduct of copper and lead smelting.

TOWER 10 ♦ a

A short steep drop off the *Forested Knoll* that goes into the *Slot* of the Bowl, is both a short, steep, enjoyable run and an avalanche path. It is so called because it passes near the 10th tower on the Lone Peak Triple chair.

TUNNEL TREES ●

Another of the runs favored by the smaller versions, this winds in the trees farther right off Mr K than the *Nameless Run*.

TURKEY TRAVERSE ♦

Taking the highest traverse long the top of the Bowl, gets to all of the lines off the South Wall. It is rather difficult as it crosses the avalanche debris dropped down from the cornice by ski patrol activity protecting the Bowl. As a result there are lots of up and down bumps, ridges, and hills.

The name comes as a description of the skiers whose heads jerk forwards and back like a turkey walking, as they bounce along the traverse.

TWILIGHT ♦

This nice little pocket in the trees is between Moonlight and Midnight on Challenger. It is frequently a place to find good snow.

TWIN TUNNELS ●

This access run goes from Blue Moon below Beacon Basin to the Pony Express lift, passing through the two tunnels.

VUARNET CLIFFS ♦ ♦

These are very steep and rocky cliffs off the Wave. To this day they hide patroller Jon "Yunce" Ueland's Vuarnet sunglasses. I was not told if he accidentally dropped them or lost them in a "yard sale". The latter is highly suspected.

WAR DANCE ♦

Steep and gnarly with lots of little trees and snow fences through the middle, the name clearly is due to all the whooping and hollering that you hear as people head down. The run is entered through a gate off *Three Forks* on the right below Elk Park. After wiggling through the little trees, War Dance opens up on to a wide, enjoyable, bumped meadow with a few scattered Lodgepoles. Blue Room and Colter's Hell are to the left into the trees, but a nice line down the Elevator Shaft is available to the left of the snow fences. The right is also skiable, but more challenging as it is narrower. The exit is onto Low Dog for the return to the Thundserwolf lift.

The fences were installed on a rock face that does not hold its snow. When the run was logged, too many trees were removed, and homeowners on Low Dog Road, just below the run, worried about the avalanche danger. Rather than gathering good snow for skiers, the fences are there to prevent avalanches. The regrowth of the little trees is a work in progress.

WAPITI ●

The green return track to the Thunderwolf and Southern Comfort areas from the top of Lone Moose and Little Dogie, is named for the elk, *Cervus canadensis*. This large member of the deer family, also called the Wapiti for "white rump", can occasionally be seen on the golf course in the summer. Not as comfortable with human activity as the moose that frequent our yards, the Big Sky elk herd tends to be more secretive and found up in the trees.

Wapiti   *Gary Zahn*

WATERFALL a

To the east of In Run and above Low Bench in the Bowl is this appropriately named avalanche path.

WAVE ♦ ♦

Riding up the Shedhorn lift, this area can be seen off to the left. The name is from the obvious shape of this cliff. Just like surfing, riding the big wave is the easy part. It is getting up on the Wave and getting off that is the challenge. Down Lenin and across Castro to get there, and the descent off the Vuarnet Cliffs make this a real double black.

WEST WALL a

As you look up from the top of the Triple chair or the Tram house, between the Little Couloir and the A Chute is a steep rock wall with a dark horizontal band through it. This is the West Wall.

WHITE FANG ●

The run goes through the trees on the left side of the Explorer chair just off White Wing, between it and Lone Wolf. There is a practice jump in here, and after a mellow trip through the trees, it drops down steep and narrow back to White Wing. Favored by small persons, parents can be startled by this drop, and this is why some locals have dubbed this a green diamond.

White Fang is the title of a classic novel by American author Jack London written in 1906. It is the story of a wild wolfdog's journey toward becoming civilized during the Klondike Gold Rush.

WHITE OTTER ● /

The name is for a lift and access trail to White Otter Road in the Cascade subdivision. There was a White Otter Crow chief alive in the 1870s, but the more famous White Otter was the boy hero of Frederic Remington's book, *The Way of an Indian*, published in

"Pretty Mother of the Night - White Otter is No Longer a Boy"
Frederic Remington, 1906

59

1906. It was the source of the story, "White Otter's Own Shadow" and the theme for the painting "Pretty Mother of the Night - White Otter is No Longer a Boy" seen here. In this coming of age and vision quest story, Remington captured the images and spirit of the Crow in the late 19th century.

Trumpeter Swan pair   *Donna Dewhurst*

WHITE WING ●

Along with Lone Wolf, this easy green comes off the Explorer chair. These two are the preferred first runs for the beginner who has graduated from the Magic Carpet. Gentle and steady, it is shaped like a wide half-pipe, making for great swooping turns up the sides.

There is no specific reference to an individual of this name, but it was intended to have a Native American sound. The wing of the white swan has been used by Native Americans as a symbol of peace. The rare trumpeter swan, *Cygnus buccinator*, is native to the nearby Madison and Henry's Fork Rivers.

WOUNDED KNEE ♦

Neither a ski injury nor a massacre, this lovely glade wanders the trees between Ambush and Hangman's. Considered one of the sweetest of the Andesite glades, it can be entered from the Andesite cat track or the Ramcharger lift line. However, the entrance through the gate from Hangman's upper right avoids the rocks that tend to form on the other two.

The bones and heart of the Sioux chief Crazy Horse were reputedly buried along Wounded Knee Creek by his family following his murder in 1877. Made famous by the 1970 book by Dee Brown, *Bury My Heart at Wounded Knee*, the name commemorates the last "battle" of the Plains Wars. On December 29, 1890, the United States 7th Cavalry killed more than 300 men, women and children, members of a Ghost Dance cult, who were being relocated to the Sioux reservation at Pine Ridge.

WYOMING BOWL ♦

Way to the right of Dakota Bowl, and coming down into Bob's Corner, this area was named by Bob Dixon and Jon "Yunce" Ueland, patrollers who explored it when it was out of bounds. Steeper than Dakota Bowl, mountainous Wyoming seemed appropriate.

YELLOW BRICK ROAD ●

This is the unofficial name given to the trail that serves the top of all the Southern Comfort runs. It starts about 100 yards below the top of Ponderosa off the Ramcharger lift, goes right, and crosses El Dorado and Sacajawea before ending up on Deep South. The Yellow Brick Road will get you to all these runs. You may also find courage... or a brain... or a heart, but it will not get you back to Kansas.

YELLOW MULE ♦

The Yellow Mule Plateau lies just south of Big Sky in the Lee Metcalf Wilderness. A hiking and horseback trail off the Ousel Falls Park trail just south of the Big Sky Town Center heads up this way. There was a ranger cabin of this name in years past. It was removed with the latest land exchange, and the Yellowstone Club, with significantly more upscale construction, is located where the cabin used to be.

The run starts skier's left of the Shedhorn lift, along with one of the Larkspur entrances and drops over a series of rollers, angling left to a flat meadow. At the end of this meadow is Middle Road which can be followed left to Dude Park. Straight ahead over the road, the run drops down a steep section to Cow Flats and the lift. This bottom part can be quite stumpy and rocky if the snow is not deep enough for good cover.

YELLOWSTONE CONFERENCE CENTER

Named for Yellowstone Park, our first and largest National Park which is just 20 miles south of Big Sky, this has become known as the premier place to host meetings in Montana.

YETI TRAVERSE ♦ ♦

A short distance down Liberty Bowl, this traverse is well marked and heads left to Marx, Lenin and the double black diamonds off of them.

Jasmine was our first avalanche dog, followed by the German Shepherds Yeti and Otter. These latter two achieved some greater fame than their predecessor as they were used for PR purposes to promote avalanche safety - the original Big Sky publicity hounds.

The Big Sky Ski Patrol uses avalanche dogs regularly for training and rescue. You may be able to see them with their handlers in the Plaza, or up by the Triple chair demonstrating their skills.

The Yeti or Abominable Snowman is a mythological creature and an ape-like cryptid said to inhabit the Himalayan region of Nepal and Tibet. It is reputed to favor Miller Lite Beer. Although carried by some boarders, beer is not necessary for Yeti protection on Lone Mountain.

YOGI'S HAT ♦

This sweet powder meadow is between Stump Farm and Chuck's Run. The entrance path is through the trees midway down Chuck's on the left. It is a narrow, winding tree-tight path and can get a bit hairy. The reward is a wide open meadow/glade that is often a secret powder stash.

It was named because it looks like the cartoon bear's hat as you look up at the meadow from the Middle Road. "Hey, there Boo Boo!" If you get to ski this secret glade you will be "Smart-ter than the av-er-age bear!"

ZUCCHINI PATCH ♦

This steep tree run to the right of the Highway was named for Gordon "Zucchini" Lehman, a patroller who skied it in the early 80s.

Follow the route above the trees off the bottom of the Country Club and turn down through the big trees parallel to the right of the Highway and the High Clearing. You will be rewarded with some steep, lovely turns.

Lone Peak, The North Side   *Moonlight Basin*

MOONLIGHT BASIN

Originally started as Moonlight Basin Ranch in 1992 as a real estate development, this opened as an independent ski area in December 2003. The first two chairlifts, Iron Horse and Pony Express were installed in the mid-1990s and were initially run by Big Sky Resort. They reverted to Moonlight Basin in 2003, but are still used today by visitors to both resorts.

Moonlight Basin boasts the longest lift in Montana, the Six Shooter, at 8700' in length and a vertical rise of 1850'. Its long, beautifully groomed cruisers are a favorite with visitors. The gladed runs off the Lone Tree lift and the steep runs in the Headwaters Area, along with the huge and truly extreme North Summit Snowfield off the top of Lone Peak are exceptional and have put Moonlight on the national map. Highly rated for its lack of crowding and customer service, it has a ski school that promotes small class size and a great kids program.

A combined pass for both Big Sky and Moonlight was first offered for the 2005-06 season. Now this has expanded and, since the promotion of The Biggest Skiing in America in 2009, the resort's 1900 acres and 92 runs have been broadened with access to to 5512 acres and over 250 official runs. With a longest run - Horseshoe - at 2.8 miles, and a drop from the summit of 4150' (did I mention the 400+ inches of powder a season?) this has become one of the great American ski experiences.

The following alphabetical list represents all the current available runs at Moonlight Basin. Those that are not on the official trail map are listed in italics. Green dots ● are the easiest, blue squares ■ are intermediate runs, and black diamonds ◆ are expert, with double black diamonds ◆◆ the extreme terrain. Please be aware that all these classes are relative, and this is big mountain skiing. In general the blues and greens at Moonlight Basin are easier than comparably rated slopes at Big Sky. However, the black diamonds and especially the double black diamonds off the Headwaters and the North Summit Snowfield are as steep as anything you will ever experience. Glade skiing at Moonlight are trees at their best. They tend to be cleared of debris and hold their snow better than any glade on the mountain. However, trees have a bad habit of not moving when you want them to, so glade skiing is a true black diamond adventure as it requires the ability to do short, tight, precise turns.

As before, all references to direction refer to the skier's right and left unless otherwise noted. That said, whether you want lovely, wide groomers, beautiful glades, or steep challenges; have a read, pick your lines, and enjoy a great day on the slopes

The daily snow report is on the Snow Phone at 406-993-6666 or online. Those interested in more information should visit www.moonlightbasin.com.

MOONLIGHT TRAILS CHECKLIST:

These represent all of the trails listed on the official Moonlight Basin trail map, as well as the unofficial named trails in italics. Trail maps are available at the ticket window and at Madison and Moonlight Lodges. They are also on the trail map section of the Moonlight Basin website.

GREEN:
- ☐ Alpine Meadows
- ☐ Buckaroo
- ☐ *Christmas Tree*
- ☐ Cinnabar
- ☐ Cupajo
- ☐ Giddy-Up
- ☐ Glacier Way
- ☐ Lazy Jack
- ☐ Natawista
- ☐ Pony Express
- ☐ Smithy
- ☐ Springville
- ☐ Stage Fright
- ☐ Twin Tunnels
- ☐ Wagon Train
- ☐ Yaak

BLUE CRUISERS:
- ☐ Blue Moon
- ☐ Coulee
- ☐ Fast Lane
- ☐ Horseshoe
- ☐ Lone Creek
- ☐ Lookout Ridge
- ☐ Meriwether
- ☐ Park Avenue
- ☐ Powder River
- ☐ Stillwater Traverse
- ☐ Trembler
- ☐ Terrain Park

REAL ESTATE ACCESS:
- ☐ Bootlegger
- ☐ Diamond Hitch
- ☐ Drover
- ☐ Gambler
- ☐ Hideaway
- ☐ Saddle Ridge

BLUE BUMPS:
- ☐ Horseshoe Bowl
- ☐ Jackrabbit
- ☐ Riffle

BLUE GLADES:
- ☐ Ice House

BLACK GLADES:
- ☐ Big Tree Cutoff
- ☐ Black Powder
- ☐ Broken Heart
- ☐ Clark's
- ☐ Double Jack
- ☐ Grizzly Meadows
- ☐ Legend
- ☐ Lone Creek Gully
- ☐ Marshal
- ☐ Moonshine
- ☐ Old Faithful
- ☐ Patrol Trees
- ☐ Ram's Glade
- ☐ Shaftway
- ☐ Single Jack
- ☐ Timber Wolf
- ☐ *Tom's Run*
- ☐ Trapline
- ☐ Ulery's Trace
- ☐ Whiskey
- ☐ White Bark

BLACK BUMPS:
- ☐ Bad Dog
- ☐ Broken Promise
- ☐ Elkhorn
- ☐ Highline
- ☐ *Highwater Traverse*
- ☐ Iron Horse
- ☐ Iron Maiden
- ☐ Lone Tree
- ☐ Obsidian
- ☐ Runaway
- ☐ Snake Bite
- ☐ Stillwater Bowl

DOUBLE BLACKS:
- ☐ Alder Gulch
- ☐ *Asteroid Rock*
- ☐ Class 4,5,6
- ☐ Cold Springs
- ☐ Dead Goat
- ☐ Deepwater Bowl
- ☐ *Don't Tell Mama*
- ☐ Double Drop
- ☐ Elbow
- ☐ Firehole
- ☐ Great Falls
- ☐ Headwaters Bowl
- ☐ Hellroaring
- ☐ Hell's Half Acre
- ☐ Jack Creek
- ☐ North Summit Snowfield
- ☐ Orbit
- ☐ RIPS
- ☐ Rock Creek
- ☐ Spillway
- ☐ Summit Direct
- ☐ Tears
- ☐ Three Forks 1,2,3
- ☐ Trident
- ☐ White Tail
- ☐ Whitewater Area

MOONLIGHT TRAIL DESCRIPTIONS

ALDER GULCH ♦♦

The first chute to the left of the Headwaters lift, Alder Gulch is double black steep, but open with good visibility. The return through the small grove of trees to the lift is obvious. Going straight at the bottom leads into Stillwater Bowl and the Lone Tree lift, or on down to the Six Shooter.

Although located in the Headwaters Bowl area, this run breaks away from the flowing waters theme and has a name that is heavy with its Montana heritage. The second gold strike in Montana Territory, Alder Gulch, was found in 1863 by Bill Fairweather and his party. Attacked by a band of Crow Indians, they hid in a gulch, where they discovered gold in the stream. Named for the Alder bushes that lined the creek, it became the site of the largest placer gold strike in history, yielding $10 million in the first year. Virginia City, home of the Vigilantes, territorial capital from 1865-75, and current seat of our Madison County is situated here. This historic site is well worth a summer visit.

ALPINE MEADOWS●

This is a service trail for the homes just to the west of Moonlight Lodge and goes from Bootlegger to Hideaway. Most alpine meadows in this area are famous for their beautiful wild flowers. This one is filled with beautiful homes instead.

ASTEROID ROCK

This wind blasted, rocky "asteroid looking" thing above the Headwaters Bowl was named in the old Nashville days by Eddie Garcia, an early patroller.

BAD DOG♦

One of the best choices for your first black diamond mogul run, this short drop off the Fast Lane is a good workout. Midway down Bad Dog, the cat track to Moonlight Lodge cuts across, giving an escape if you are getting beat up by the bumps. Continuing down the moguls leads to the bottom of Riffle and on to the Iron Horse lift. Be careful that the bad dog doesn't jump up and grab your leg.

BEACON BASIN

In the open meadow below Blue Moon and above the Diamond Hitch subdivision, the people of Moonlight Basin and Backcountry Access have constructed a park to practice your beacon and probe skills. Several transceivers are buried about in simulated avalanche debris and can be activated from the central post.

Wearing a beacon or transceiver on your body in the "send" mode is only smart when skiing in avalanche country. Carrying a shovel and probe, and knowing how to use the transceiver in "search" mode can be critical if your buddy is buried.

BIG TREE CUTOFF ♦

This is a good place to demonstrate your mogul technique... or lack thereof. It is entered from the sign on the Stillwater Traverse near the Lone Tree lift, or from the bottom of Lone Tree (N) by angling left near the base of the lift. It continues down bumps and open trees to join Broken Heart and Marshall into Meriwether and on to the Six Shooter. The name comes from the big tree - in the midst of many.

BLACK POWDER ♦

One of the early glades cut at Moonlight, and still on the trail maps, this is no longer a run. The trail sign has been removed and snow fences placed at the entrance off Wagon Train. As it went off the Derringer beginner area, and was a black diamond of poor quality, it was not appropriate here.

This run did not hold its snow well, and skiing it caused one to go poof! like black powder.

BLAZING SADDLES SLEDDING HILL

Blazing Saddles was a 1974 Mel Brooks satirical comedy of the Old West. It was a fun movie and this is a fun sledding hill.

BLUE MOON ■

Moon from Moonlight and a blue square run make this an appropriate name for this mellow, well groomed run. Take the Fast Lane from the top of the Six Shooter or the Iron Horse lifts past Bad Dog and onto the lower slopes of Challenger. Blue Moon is the groomed section down the valley that angles left above the Diamond Hitch subdivision homes and down to the base of the Iron Horse lift.

Rogers & Hart wrote the song in1933, "Blue moon/you saw me standing alone/without a dream in my heart/without a love of my own". It has been sung by Mel Torme, Elvis Presley, Bob Dylan, Eric Clapton, and most famously by the Marcels. The song bridges all ages, and like this run, is great whatever your age.

BOOTLEGGER ●

This trail is actually an access to Cowboy Heaven that was given a western themed name. Bootlegger means the making, transporting and/or selling illegal alcoholic liquor. The term originates from concealing hip flasks of alcohol in the legging of boots. Stills have not been found in the woods of Cowboy Heaven, and the Revenooers should give you no trouble here.

BROKEN HEART ♦

A broken heart, when a human being suffers from an emotional or physical loss, is just a name; but what a lovely run.

This is often the first black diamond for advanced intermediates to try for relatively easy trees and moguls. In the early season, rocks can be exposed, because of the pitch and wind. However, after the coverage develops, it can be wonderful. The easiest line is with a hard right off the Lone Tree lift onto the open knob and down along the edge of Patrol Trees, keeping them on your left. The more difficult line is to follow Lone Tree North under the lift, then left at the trees. The return to the Lone Tree lift follows a blue track to your right, but going left to the trail into the trees, leads to the more difficult, but interesting glade. The trees are rather open in this section, and the bottom connects with the Big Tree Cutoff and on into Meriwether, for a cruise back to the Six-Shooter.

BROKEN PROMISE ♦

This run, left off the lower portion of Lookout Ridge, starts as a lovely little run, like one finds in eastern ski areas. It just ends at the bottom of a hill that you will need to hike up... thus the "broken promise" Best avoided unless the sweetness of the powder lures you into justifying a wearisome climb.

BUCKAROO●

The term comes from the Spanish word vaquero meaning cowboy. It is now generally used as an affectionate term for young boys. Riding the Derringer lift, you can see these buckaroos as they schuss by off Stage Fright.

CEDAR MOUNTAIN CORRAL

This beautiful mountain at 10,800 feet lies just to the south of Lone Mountain in the Lee Metcalf Wilderness. Although Lone Mountain blocks the view of this peak from Moonlight Basin, it can be seen off the top of the Thunderwolf chair at Big Sky, or from the top of the Tram and the North Summit Snowfield. The summer hike to Cedar Mountain from Moonlight is rewarded by a view of Cedar Creek that has a free fall of nearly 1000'.

CHRISTMAS TREE ●

This is a favorite of the kids and was named by them. It starts off Cinnabar after crossing the bridge. Keep way right and follow the trees to Drover. Your children or grandchildren will appreciate the gift of leading them down this run.

CINNABAR ●

This is a western name full of the spirit of mining in this area. On the early trail maps this was Wagon Train, but the names were switched early on so that people could follow this one run from the top of the Six-Shooter lift to the Madison Lodge.

The Devil's Slide, a red striped avalanche chute in the Paradise Valley, *Devil's Slide*   *Mike Cline*

just east of here, was reportedly so colored by the devil's rear as he slid down the mountain. It is actually cinnabar. This common sulfide ore of mercury has been mined since Neolithic times for the red pigment and the metal. Its presence is associated with recent volcanic activity.

CLARK'S ♦

This is the first glade you will come to on the right off Horseshoe. Short and steep, it drops into the flats of Trembler for the return. If you want to stay off the groomers, you can enter Grizzly Meadows at the bottom of Clark's for more trees. This run was cut in the 3rd or 4th summer of Moonlight Basin during the Lewis and Clark Bicentennial celebration, so the name appeared appropriate.

William Clark (August 1, 1770 – September 1, 1838) along with Meriwether Lewis, led the Corps of Discovery now known as the Lewis and Clark Expedition from 1803 to 1805 across the Louisiana Purchase to the Pacific Ocean and back. He passed close to Big Sky via Three Forks on the way west and through Bozeman coming back. After his return he served as

William Clark, 1810 Charles Willson Peal

governor of the Missouri Territory, and from 1822 until his death he held the position of Superintendent of Indian Affairs.

Many western names come from this explorer. The cutthroat trout *(Oncorhynchus clarki)* and Clark's Nutcracker *(Nucifraga columbiana)* are familiar to many. Helena is the seat of Lewis and Clark County, the Clark Fork River near Missoula, and the Clarks Fork of the Yellowstone River were both named for him.

CLASS 4, 5, 6 ♦ ♦
(See Whitewater)

Most of the chutes of the Headwaters have a water related name and these come from the classification of river rapids for whitewater kayaking, canoeing or rafting. The American Whitewater Affiliation lists a Class 4 rapids as "Intense, powerful, but predictable rapids requiring precise boat handling... demanding fast maneuvers under pressure." Class 5 are "Extremely long, obstructed or very violent rapids which expose a paddler to above average endangerment. Drops may contain... congested chutes with complex, demanding routes." Class 6, labeled "Extreme and Exploratory ...have almost never been attempted and often exemplify the extremes of difficulty, unpredictability and danger. The consequences of error are very severe...". You should know that there is probably a good reason why these chutes, way left on the Headwaters and above the rock band, were so named.

In the old Nashville Bowl era, before Moonlight, these chutes represented the V in "Elvis"

COLD SPRINGS ♦ ♦

To skier's left of Alder Gulch, this is one of the four good skiable chutes in the Headwaters. It is recognizable for the big wind lip that forms on the left side of the chute. Opening into Stillwater Bowl, you can cut across the bottom of Alder Gulch to get a return lap up the Headwaters lift.

Again, this fits with the names of the Headwaters chutes being water related. There is a true spring visible in summer at the base of the cliffs.

COULEE ■

Running along the Six Shooter lift, this is an alternate blue groomer off Meriwether to get to the base of the lift. Coulee is the common western pronunciation of couloir, a deep mountain gorge or gully. It comes from the French couler meaning to slide or flow and pronounces coulee. Although this intermediate run is in no way a steep couloir, it does have a western flavor. It also has an interesting derivation. The group that originally named the runs at Moonlight Basin, led by General Manager Burt Mills, wanted to honor the founders of the ski area. These men did not feel that their names should be on the runs, so this is how Lee Poole is memorialized at Moonlight Basin.

Lee Poole and Joe Vujovich   *Moonlight Basin*

CUPAJO ●

Sometimes pronounced Koo-pa'-ho, this is no real Spanish word. It may have been derived from the song "Cupajoe" by the heavy metal band Anthrax, released in 1998. Certainly skiing can give you a sensation greater than a caffeine rush. Actually, again, this is a tribute to one of the founders of Moonlight Basin, Joe Vujovich, who also didn't want his actual name used on any of the runs. Take this run from the Derringer area to Madison Lodge for a warm-up and a Cup of Joe.

DEAD GOAT ♦ ♦

A short climb up left from the top of the Lone Tree lift gets to the traverse leading to Lone Tree South, Obsidian, and Dead Goat chutes. All are steep double black diamond runs, but the easiest entries into the western upper Stillwater Bowl area. Like the runs off the Headwaters lift, these chutes can be lapped with little delay, using the Lone Tree lift.

The run's name deviates from the usual naming of Headwaters gullies with water related monikers. This is because of a real event that occurred

Mountain Goat   Dave Grickson,

here in the early 90s. Patrollers saw a huge late season avalanche down this gully. Goat tracks were seen going into the slide, but none came out. The following summer, a goat carcass was found by hikers at the base of the slide.

As if to reinforce this name, in 2005 some skiers traversing into the area frightened a herd of mountain goats and a kid spooked and fell off the cliff. Patroller, Troy Howe, did CPR on the goat and revived it. It was taken out on a ski patrol sled, but later died of the injuries. The legend that a skier hit the goat and both were injured seems not to be true.

DEEPWATER BOWL ♦ ♦

Found at the bottom of Great Falls and RIPs off the North Summit Snowfield, some great lines can be had in the powder that collects in this bowl.
At GM Burt Mills suggestion, this is a play off the Whitewater/Stillwater areas in the Headwaters Bowl on the other side. It was originally called Deepwater Wild, but the "Wild" was dropped as being too "Disney".

Derringer

DERRINGER/

This lift serves the beginner area and Madison Lodge. Being small, it serves a nice partner to its big brother, the Six Shooter lift. The term derringer is a misspelling of the last name of Henry Deringer, a famous maker of small pocket pistols in the 1800s. With many copies of the original Philadelphia Deringer the name was often misspelled This misspelling soon became a generic term for any pocket pistol

DIAMOND HITCH●

The name for this subdivision below Blue Moon and the Madison Lodge and the feeder track to it comes from the traditional western tie used to attach gear to the pack saddle on a horse or mule. It was invented by the Spanish in Mexico and introduced to the U.S. Cavalry 1879.

DON'T TELL MAMA ♦ ♦

Located between Obsidian and Dead Goat in the Headwaters on the short hike above the Lone Tree lift, this sweet line deserves a name of its own.

Named by Randy Spence, this terrain was originally off limits before the construction of the Lone Tree lift. When it was first skied, it was so sweet that the skiers all looked at each other and said "don't tell Mama!".

DOUBLE-JACK ♦

One of the loveliest tree runs at Moonlight, Double Jack is entered off Lookout Ridge on the right after the flats. It is a long run through the trees with alternating areas of

Double Jack

steeps and flats that will often have soft powder a couple days after the storm. Keep to the left in the trees as Ulery's Trace and Trapline have the same entrance.

Double Jack is a mining term for a two handed sledge hammer with a 36 inch handle and 6-8 pound head. It is the tool that John Henry used in the song of the "steel drivin' man". The government publication from the U S Department of Transportation says that "these require considerable expertise from both the driller and holder, we recommend that you use single jacking or modified double jacking until safety and proficiency with the double jack can be assured." This is not to say, however, that you should only ski Single Jack until you are more proficient, just don't hit your holder.

DROVER ●

This run is like herding cows, flat and slow. Coming off Bootlegger to Cinnabar, it serves primarily as a way for people staying in the homes near Moonlight Lodge to get to the Six Shooter lift.

ELBOW ♦ ♦

Coming down off of the Three Forks the trail makes an elbow turn to the right. It's nice and wide so there is lots of elbow room. (Note that "nice and wide" is a term for this double black that came from those young skiers that climbed up to ski the cliffs of Three Forks!)

ELKHORN ♦

Suitable for advanced intermediates, this should be your first black diamond experience. Wide, with small regular moguls, this is steep only for the first couple hundred yards. Thereafter, it mellows to a blue cruiser back to the Six-Shooter. Please do not think that if you can handle this black diamond that you can do the Headwaters, which are several degrees of difficulty above this.

This area was used by Montana Backcountry Adventures for cat skiing before the development of Moonlight Basin. Then it was called "Phantom", but Elkhorn fits more in the western theme. The elk actually has an antler that is shed yearly, rather than a true horn, but the term has stuck. (pun)

There are many place names of Elkhorn in the west, but the most familiar in Montana is the ghost town in the Elkhorn Mountains SE of the town of Boulder off Montana Highway 69. There was a huge silver strike here in the late 1800s and at one time three railroads served the town. A diphtheria epidemic killed all of the children in the town in 1887, and when silver went bust the next year, the town disappeared. The historic Miner's Hall, cemetery, and several remaining buildings make an interesting visit.

FAST LANE ■

This was named because it is the direct route back to the Big Sky base area from the Six-Shooter and Iron Horse lifts. It has a fairly fast descent for a track, thus the blue square and name. Use it to access the Iron Horse runs like Blue Moon, Bad Dog and Powder River.

FIREHOLE ♦ ♦

Fourth of the good skiable chutes off the Headwaters lift, this run is to the left of Cold Spring. It, too, enters the Stillwater Bowl, but Headwaters laps are possible if you cut back across the bottom of Cold Spring and Alder Gulch.

This route down the Headwaters was originally called Second Graceland in the Elvis inspired out of bounds Nashville Bowl before Moonlight Basin existed. The present name, echoing the river theme in the Headwaters, is for the Firehole River in Yellowstone Park. Named for the numerous thermal features along its route, the Firehole joins the Gibbon River at Madison Junction to form the Madison River.

GAMBLER ●

Connecting Cinnabar with the Pony Express, this is an easy green through the residential district. Having nothing to do with Kenny Rodgers, it is just a western themed name. All true western B movies have a character of the poker playing gambler, but as a green run, it is not much of a gamble to take. Just don't hold Aces and eights!

GIDDY-UP ●

From the older English Get ye up!, a command to start a horse moving. On this little green glade under the Derringer lift between Cinnabar and Stage Fright, no one will need to tell the young skiers here to Giddy Up.

GLACIER WAY ●

Again, this is a western themed name for this short run off the top of the Derringer lift to Wagon Train. Glacier Park in NW Montana is called the Crown Jewel of the Continent.

GREAT FALLS ♦ ♦

This is the more difficult of two very steep runs off the North Summit Snowfield. Access requires a trip up the Tram at Big Sky and a sign-out with the Moonlight Ski patrol. Probe, shovel, transceiver and a buddy are also mandatory.

Named for the falls of the Missouri that hindered Lewis and Clark, the nearby city of Great Falls is the commercial hub of North Central Montana. The fact that this run is a steep fall off the North Summit Snow Field makes the name even more appropriate. Boats are discouraged down this cataract.

GRIZZLY MEADOWS ♦

Grizzly in Yellowstone   Terry Tollefsbol

This run is worth exploring, but not on the "A" list. With so many great tree runs at Moonlight Basin, it is hard to recommend this particular glade off the left side of Trembler. There was strong bear sign in this glade when it was cut, and with this large bear common in Yellowstone and near Moonlight Basin, the name was appropriate. Also, the University of Montana sports mascot and team name is the Grizzly. Go Griz!!

HEADWATERS BOWL ♦ ♦ /

Before the days of Moonlight Basin, this area was out of bounds off the Challenger chair and was called Nashville Bowl. At that time, the locals, following the lead of Sam Wilson, had names for the various chutes that followed an Elvis theme. With a great amount of imagination, looking up at the rocks, one could see the name Elvis spelled out.

Since it is the headwaters of the Jack Creek drainage that flows through Moonlight to the Madison River near Ennis, MT, that name seemed more appropriate. The chutes have all been renamed by Moonlight Basin, and they now mostly follow on a waters of Montana theme.

Sequins on his parka notwithstanding, there is no truth to the rumor that the King is alive and shredding the Headwaters.

Headwaters   *Moonlight Basin*

74

HELLROARING ♦ ♦

Difficult, steep, and rocky; this very technical descent is to the left of the "good" Headwaters chutes. Hellroaring is a western name common to many creeks. The nearest is north of Big Sky in US 191 at milepost 63. This trail, just south of Storm Castle, can be followed south through the Spanish Peaks section of the Lee Metcalf Wilderness, over the pass by Summit Lake, and down to Big Sky through Bear Basin.

HELL'S HALF ACRE ♦ ♦

The next line left of Hellroaring in the Headwaters was closed when it was managed by Big Sky. After it was acquired by Moonlight Basin it was explored and deemed skiable. The run is less than great, very steep and rocky, and thus the name.

The geographic Hell's Half Acre is on the upper reaches of the South Fork of the Powder River in eastern Wyoming. It is a bizarrely wind modeled badlands, and bizarre is a good term for anyone wanting to ski this.

HIDEAWAY●

A short service trail to homes off Natawista is used to get to your little hideaway in the woods at Moonlight.

HIGHLINE ♦

Dropping off the top of the Six-Shooter towards Meriwether and the base of the Lone Tree lift, this black diamond gives a bit of a challenge to the usual Stillwater Traverse. Next to, or in the trees, it can be nice in good snow. Clearly a black diamond, it makes an interesting, often empty alternative to the mob of people heading down Stillwater Traverse.

Although this is a high line, or route, off the mountain, it is actually a logging term representing a cable device for dragging timber out of the woods. It is rather like a Zip Line for logs, allowing them to be moved downhill or over streams with less effort. A spar tree was guyed up with the cable on top and logs were attached to it to slide on the cable down and off the hill. It had little eco-impact or road-building.

HIGHWATER TRAVERSE ♦

This traverse in the Headwaters area goes below the rock band along the top of Stillwater Bowl and well above the Stillwater Traverse. It provides access to all the lines in this bowl below the crazy parts of Hellroaring, Jack and Rock Creek, and the Whitewater sections. Since these runs carry the theme of stream names, it is indeed a high water traverse.

However, if this really was "the high water mark", a search should be made for the Ark.

HORSESHOE ■

Named for the shape of this run that swings around the western edge of Moonlight Basin, it is an easy blue. Always well groomed, it is one of the longest runs on all of Lone Mountain - a total of 2.8 miles. At 25 degrees of slope, it qualifies as a blue run, but is one of the easier ones. It is a good run to start on when you move up to blues, and has, in addition, excellent views of Fan Mountain to the west and Spanish Peaks to the north.

Horseshoe   *Man Vyi*

HORSESHOE BOWL■

Above and left of the top of the Lone Tree lift, this nice bowl drops into the Horseshoe run. A little climb can result in great powder. A horseshoe is supposed to bring good luck. It is your good luck to be skiing this bowl with the excellent snow and views.

ICE HOUSE ■

Coming off Lookout Ridge to the right, Moonshine, Marshall, and Ice House start together. Ungroomed, but of moderate pitch, and few trees, this makes a good start to glade skiing. It also serves as an escape if your skill does not match your ego when you started down Moonshine or Ulery's.

When this glade was cut, the loggers found glacial ice below the rock. They said that it would be a great place for an ice house to keep the beer cold.

IRON HORSE/♦

This lift was built 1994 and comes from the Indian name for a locomotive. Installed by Moonlight Basin, it was initially managed by Big Sky. It reverted to Moonlight Basin when this ski resort opened in 2003, but lift tickets from both resorts work here. With "The Biggest Skiing in America", it now provides a joint interconnection to these two great ski areas and allows access to 5500 acres of fun at both.

The Iron Horse run on the trail map is a cat track connecting Powder River and Iron Maiden. It is listed as a black diamond because there is no easy way out.

IRON MAIDEN♦

The run descends along a narrow, mogully pitch under the Iron Horse lift, ending at the cat track to Moonlight Lodge. A challenging run suitable for an advanced intermediate, this can be great with deep, fresh snow. However, the presence of rocks and stumps, and the need for short turns in this narrow run, can make it very difficult with low snow.

An iron maiden is a torture device, consisting of an iron cabinet, with a hinged front, like a mummy case. It usually had a small closeable opening so that the torturer could interrogate the victim and holes to allow piercing the body with knives, spikes or nails. Without good snow, the rocks and stumps do make this run a bit of a torture device. However, with powder, she can be a very sweet maiden.

JACK CREEK ♦ ♦

One of the Headwaters chutes to the left of Hell's Half Acre, this is steep, rocky, and not recommended. Moonlight Basin lies in the drainage of Jack Creek that flows from the Headwaters to join the Madison River near Ennis, MT. Named after the body of a dead jackass was found on the banks of the creek, the name was subsequently shortened to Jack.

Jackass   *Adrian Pingstone*

JACKASS CREEK SALOON

A jackass is a male donkey or ass. Used for 3000 years as a beast of burden, the donkey or burro was a favorite of the grubstake prospectors.

Jackrabbit   *Dean Biggins*

JACK RABBIT ■

Most jackrabbits are found farther south in the US in desert or chaparral country, but the Blacktail is present in Yellowstone National Park. It, too has the distinctive long ears, and the long, powerful rear legs characteristic of hares. This is a fun run off the cat track off the top of the Lone Tree lift on down to Trembler. Where is that wascally wabbit?

LAZY JACK ●

The easy green run off the top of the Six-Shooter lift was named for the way it lazes its way down the mountain. It was not named for any particular person, even if you know him.

It fits with Double and Single Jack names, but lazy jacks are not a hammer, but a nautical term for a type of rigging which assists in sail handling during reefing and furling. It is generally claimed that the name has its origins in the colloquial reference to British sailors as "Jack tars".

LEGEND ♦

This short glade from Horseshoe to Trembler is between Clark's and Old Faithful. Your skill in here is the stuff of which legends are made.

LONE CREEK ■ GULLY ♦

These two runs are named for the creek that follows the bottom of this narrow gully from the base of the Lone Tree lift. Lone Creek, the blue run, is the more civilized route to the right off Meriwether where Big Tree Cutoff and Broken Heart come in. It is well groomed and reenters Meriwether to return to the Six Shooter. The Gully run is favored by young snowboarders and skied by the unsuspecting. A narrow half-pipe at the beginning, it gets narrower, and the trees get thicker as one descends. There is no real escape, so you end up a creek.

LONE TREE / ♦ and ♦ ♦

The lift, and the run under it, were named for the single pine that stands on this ridge above everything else. The lift provides access to the whole raft of cruiser runs to the west of the Six Shooter as well as some great glades.

Of the runs named for the lift, Lone Tree North♦, skier's left of the lift, is the easier line as it is more open and runs along with Broken Heart. Where the latter veers left into the trees and on down to the Six Shooter, Lone Tree North goes straight along the lift line for a return lap. Lone Tree♦ follows directly under the lift and Lone Tree South ♦ ♦ does the trees to the skier's right of the lift. Although labeled as single black diamonds, these are among the more difficult, and should only be skied by those with skill in steep bumps and trees. You are also visible to everyone on the lift, so be ready to show off, or to absorb derogatory comments. Brainless descents or spectacular falls will, however, get high point ratings.

LOOKOUT RIDGE ■

The run is a smooth, mellow blue cruiser, well suited as an intermediate choice. The entry is via the wide track past the patrol shack as you exit the Lone Tree lift. Upon entering Horseshoe Bowl, be sure to keep hard right on the first cat track that leads to this run. An alternate, more difficult approach, is through the short, but steep and tight Patrol Trees. After the entrance, all is mellow, and the views spectacular.

In addition to being the access to the best glades at Moonlight Basin, and with great views, it is a good trip to take with your real estate agent.

MARSHAL ♦

Entered along with Ice House off the right of Lookout Ridge, you will need to stay more to the right for some nice steep tree skiing that goes on to the bottom of Broken Heart and Big Tree Cutoff.

Very western, the town marshal was the "Good Guy" like Matt Dillon of Gunsmoke. The term comes from the old French name Marecheaux given to an ancient court of justice in Paris called the "Tribunal of Constables and Marshals of France". Be sure to behave and wear your white hat when you ski in here.

MERIWETHER ■

The main blue run off the top of the Six Shooter to the base, this trail is smooth, consistently groomed, and very mellow. It is a pleasure for anyone to ski.

Named for Capt. Meriwether Lewis (August 18, 1774 – October 11, 1809), who, along with William Clark led the Corps of Discovery up the Missouri and over to the Columbia to the Pacific coast and back in 1804-06. He passed as close to Moonlight Basin as the town Three Forks, some 30 miles NW. Lewis is credited with naming our major rivers, the Gallatin, Madison, and Jefferson after the president and the Secretaries of Treasury and State sitting in 1804. Meriwether campground in the Gates of the Mountains just north of Helena

Meriwether Lewis
Charles Willson Peale

off I-90 was a site of the expedition's camp and well worth the boat trip to visit. Lewis and Clark Caverns above the Jefferson River on Highway 287 south of Three Forks was never visited by the Corps of Discovery, although they passed nearby. It is now a state park and has an interesting summer tour.

MOONSHINE ♦

One of the steeper tree runs off Lookout Ridge, it starts with Icehouse and Marshall. It has an advantage of paralleling Ice House, which allows a blue escape route if Moonshine seems too steep or tight.

Moonshine is a common name for illicitly distilled liquor. It was so called because it was distributed clandestinely, "by the light of the moon". Jake Ulery is reputed to have made moonshine in this area around 1910 so the name has a bit of a western and local flavor while incorporating the Moonlight Basin name.

NATAWISTA ●

Named for Natawista Culbertson (ca.1825 - 1895), who was probably, after the legendary Sacajawea, the most important Native American woman in Montana. Also known as Natoyist-Siksina, or Sacred Snake Woman, she was a daughter of Two Suns, chief of the Blood sub -tribe of the Blackfoot Nation. She was married to Alexander Culbertson who was the chief trader for the American Fur Company. During their nearly thirty years on the Upper Missouri, Natawista worked as a diplomat, a hostess, and an interpreter; helping to bridge the gap between the white traders and the native inhabitants of that region. Known as a peacemaker, she not only assisted in the fur

Natawista Culbertson
True West Magazine

trade, but also helped negotiate safe passage for the Northern Pacific railroad crews. The Culbertsons retired to Peoria, Illinois in 1858, then 10 years later came back to Montana and settled in Ft. Benton. Natawista died in 1895 in the Blood camps in Alberta. She is one of the few women with her own entry in the Dictionary of Canadian Biography.

Enjoy this easy, peaceful run that goes off Cinnabar for a delightful alternative return to Madison Lodge.

Pat Daigle on the North Summit　　　*Lonnie Ball*
courtesy Moonlight Basin

NORTH SUMMIT SNOWFIELD ♦ ♦

One of the finest steeps on the mountain, or anywhere for that matter, the extreme descents are a challenge to any skier. A sign out with the Moonlight ski patrol at the summit hut is required, as is a transceiver, probe, and shovel. For safety, only groups of 2-4 may go, and only at designated intervals. Guide service to this area is available through the Snow Sports School and is recommended for first trips. The name is obvious looking at the summit from the Moonlight Basin side, as snow remains throughout the summer.

OBSIDIAN ♦ ♦

Just to skier's right from Lone Tree South and up a short hike, this steep open glade has some great lines. Obsidian is volcanic glass that forms when lava cools quickly without crystal formation. Rather common in Montana, it was used more often that flint for arrowheads by early peoples. Obsidian Cliff nine miles north of Norris Junction in Yellowstone Park has one of the largest deposits in the country. It apparently formed when molten lava came up against glacial ice and cooled quickly. Just south of Helena near Montana City is an archeological site where there is evidence that obsidian has been quarried for several thousand years.

OLD FAITHFUL♦

Another of the short, steep glades off the top of Horseshoe, this one drops off into Grizzly Meadows. Named for the famous geyser in our neighboring Yellowstone Park, this run is one to spout off about if you do it well.

Old Faithful　　　*Jon Sullivan*

80

ORBIT♦ ♦

This is an extreme line above Deepwater Bowl and below the North Summit rock band. Named for the shape of this round patch of snow, it is skiable only after a hike up from Deepwater Bowl.

PARK AVENUE ■

The wide boulevard in Manhattan, NY gives name to this easy, groomed "street" that leads from Elkhorn into the Terrain Park. Get it? "Park" Avenue.

PATROL TREES ♦

A short drop through the rather tight trees behind the ski patrol hut at the top of the Lone Tree lift leads to Lookout Ridge. Sometimes rocky, there are interesting lines and it avoids the cat track to Lookout that goes around the knob past Horseshoe and Trembler.

PONY EXPRESS ● /

This lift was Installed 1995 and named by Big Sky at that time. Used by both resorts, Moonlight Basin now operates the Pony Express base area, as well as the beginner's Pony Terrain Park.

The pony express was noted for the speed that it delivered the mail from St Louis to California in the days before the railroads crossed the country. Perhaps the name of this lift comes more from the "pony" than the "express".

Pony Express   USPS stamps

POWDER RIVER ■

In extreme southeastern Montana, Powder River county, with Broadus the county seat, has a huge population of 1850 souls. It is name comes from the Powder River that flows north through here to join the Yellowstone some 50 miles south of Miles City. Although some feel that the river was named for its naturally muddy condition that settlers said was "too thin to plow and too thick to drink", it was actually named by Wm Clark in 1805 for the sand along the banks that resembled gunpowder. The lonely upper reaches are the site of the Hole-in-the-Wall hideout of Butch Cassidy and the Sundance Kid's Wild Bunch Gang, and the geologic oddity, Hell's Half Acre. The Powder River Basin is now a major source of low-sulfur coal.Gentle and ambling, this run to the left of the Iron Horse lift resembles the river.

RAM'S GLADE ♦

This glade, created in the early days of Moonlight Basin, does not have great skiing. Off the top of the Six-Shooter lift between Runaway and Highline, this route to the Lone Tree lift is tight and best with really good snow.

Bighorn Sheep   Ryan Hagerty

Named for the Rocky Mountain Bighorn Sheep *Ovis canadensis*, the ram is the male, and is remarkable for the huge curved horns.. A herd can often be seen on the Lone Mountain Trail spur road on the north side just up from the Conoco station.

RIFFLE ■

A short bit of moguls was cut to the right off Powder River for some variation. It drops under the Iron Horse lift and across the cat track to Moonlight Lodge, before entering the run-out of Bad Dog and back to the lift.

A riffle is a shallow stretch of a river or stream, where the swifter current forms small rippled waves. It is probably a good name for this mogulled portion of an otherwise Class I run.

RIPS ♦ ♦

Along with Great Falls, this is one of the main descents off the North Summit Snowfield, and the one most people prefer. Neither of these can be deemed "easier" as both are double black extreme runs.

This steep chute's name stands for R.I.P., and that is what we will put on your tombstone if you fall. It is not for your ripping fast speed or the damage to your clothing as you find the rocks.

ROCK CREEK ♦ ♦

Between Class 6 of the Whitewater and Jack Creek, this very steep chute has rock bands and is not recommended unless you have dad buying your skis and your health insurance is paid up.

In the theme of water and Montana that was used for the routes off the Headwaters, this one was named for the Rock Creek, near Phillpsburg MT, a prime trout stream. If you try this route, let us hope that you are neither up the creek nor on the rocks. Rather, do it from the Highwater Traverse below the rock band and you will hook a good one and enjoy.

RUNAWAY ♦

Like a runaway train you can get some speed on this easier of the Moonlight Basin black diamonds. Directly under the Six-Shooter lift, this run descends into the Terrain Park. Because of the location and the wind direction, there can be some exposed rocks, so care is indicated. During low snow times a run down Elkhorn would be a better black diamond choice.

SADDLE RIDGE

A saddle ridge is named for the familiar concave shape of a horse's saddle. Seen as a low slope along a ridge it is the usual route of a crossing trail. These condominiums on the ridge north of Moonlight Lodge are among the nicest in the area.

SHAFTWAY ♦

In mining, this is the vertical passageway leading to the surface. More recently, the word is used in architecture as in an elevator shaft. Either way you will be dealing with a steep narrow drop. This first trail to the right and through the trees off Lookout Ridge is indeed steep and narrow. It can be interesting, but there are better glades.

SINGLE-JACK ♦

This is another mining term referring to a sledge hammer held in one hand. A single jack has a three or four pound head and a ten inch handle. The miner would hold the drilling steel in one hand and use the hammer with the other. The short handle resists breaking better than the longer handled hammers, and allows for better striking accuracy. The pneumatic and noisy jackhammer that you see and hear on construction sites gets its name from this hand tool, and has largely replaced it in the mines and building trades.

Single Jack

This delightful dance through the trees off Lookout Ridge, about half way down, is just past Double Jack. It is one of the recommended first black diamond tree runs for you to try.

SIX-SHOOTER /

This lift carries six riders at a time. At 8700 feet in length and rising 1850 vertical feet, this is the longest ski lift in Montana. Serving the main runs of Moonlight Basin, it is an appropriate big brother to the little Derringer lift that serves the beginner area and Madison Lodge.

Six Shooter   Mike Cumpston

Samuel Colt patented the first "revolving gun" in 1836. It had a rotating cylinder with six chambers that moved via the hammer cock to align the next chamber with the barrel, thus the nicknames, revolver and six-shooter.

SMITHY ●

The blacksmith's forge was called a smithy. A short green diversion off Natawista, this is not the run to make a lot of smoke and fire.

SNAKE BITE ♦

Running parallel to Elkhorn off the cat track west from Iron Horse or via Lazy Jack from the Six Shooter, this trail is steep and full of moguls. It can also be full of the legendary snow snakes that are used as an excuse for falling.

A bar drink that is traditionally half and half Stout Beer and Hard Cider, it also has recipes listed as Jack Daniel's, Tequila and Tabasco; or Vodka, Green

Chartreuse and Tabasco. Whatever you mix, this run can make you feel like you have had (or need) several.

SOUTH SIDE ROAD ●

This is listed on the map as the "Emergency Access Route". It was originally a logging road and is not skiable. It is important to the groomers and ski patrol to get the cats and emergency snowmobiles around the mountain.

SPILLWAY ♦ ♦

The exit from Deepwater Bowl onto Horseshoe is Spillway. Full of trees, the pitch is significantly less awesome than the North Summit Snowfield and its exit chutes that you just came down.

A spillway is the channel that allows for a controlled release from a dam. This is a very appropriate name for this release from the North Summit.

SPRINGVILLE ●

The first right off the top of the Derringer lift, Springville leads to Cinnabar and Madison Lodge. The name comes from the many springs found here in the summer.

STAGE FRIGHT ●

A Western connotation because of the stage coach, stage fright actually refers to performance anxiety. This run goes directly under the Derringer lift, causing beginners to perform directly below an audience and experience "stage fright".

STILLWATER BOWL ♦ TRAVERSE ■

Most of the double black chutes off of the Headwaters drop into this bowl for some nice open powder at an easier pitch. Obsidian and Dead Goat off the Lone Tree lift and Cold Springs and Alder Gulch from the Headwaters lift make the best access. The lower section can also be skied from the top of the Six-Shooter lift with a bit of a climb above the Stillwater Traverse. Rarely skied, this bowl can hold some nice powder lines.

The Stillwater Traverse itself provides the easy route from the top of the Six Shooter lift, across the bowl to Meriwether and the Lone Tree lift.

With the water theme in the Headwaters, this also has a Montana allusion. The Stillwater River comes out of the Beartooth Mountains in south central Montana near Columbus and flows into the Yellowstone. It is a roaring mountain stream and in no way "still". However its name is from the Crow Indians who tell a tragic story of two lovers who died in each others' arms in the swift water. Where the bodies came to rest was called a "hallowed" place and this was mistranslated as "still".

SUMMIT DIRECT ♦ ♦

Following skier's right down from the North Summit Snowfield will bring you to a short, but narrow. opening in the rocks that leads to the direct line from the North Summit to Deepwater Bowl.

TEARS ♦♦

Between Rips and Summit Direct, this chute off the North Summit Snowfield leads to sweet open lines on Deepwater Bowl. As nice as this can be with fresh snow, there is no way that it will bring tears to your eyes. Rather it is for what can happen to your pants, along with the rips, if you fall in the early season rocks. On the other hand, the steep slope allows you to tear down with speed. Hmmm... homonomy.

THREE FORKS 1, 2, 3 ♦♦

The Three Forks of the Missouri come together 40 miles east of Bozeman and were named by Lewis & Clark for president Thomas Jefferson, his Sec of State, James Madison, and the Sec of the Treasury, Albert Gallatin. Names of rivers fit with the Headwaters theme of water in the Headwaters Bowl area. These three runs were originally the S in ELVIS during the Nashville Bowl out of bounds Graceland days. It was split into 1, 2, and 3 to denote separate chutes for the ski patrol's avalanche control. It is a climb to get there, and a very steep and difficult descent. Skill with extreme skiing is essential.

TIMBER WOLF♦

A narrow glade from Horseshoe down into Trembler meets the bottom of Grizzly Meadows. - an appropriate junction for the two major carnivores in our area. The Grey or Timber Wolf, *Canis lupus*, is the largest member of the dog family. Once exterminated from Montana as a pest to livestock, it has recently been reintroduced into the Yellowstone ecosystem to great success ... for the wolves. Our local wolves are the Cougar Pack which roams the Park

Cool Wolf   *Hans Strickler*

between Specimen Creek and the Bighorn Pass, and the Taylor Peak Pack, found west of #191 just south of Big Sky. Several sightings of a lone black wolf as well as other pack members in the Meadow Village means that these creatures are now a part of us.

TOM'S RUN ♦

Not named officially, and not really a run, locals will come off Broken Heart to Big Tree Cutoff, then left into the trees and up an unofficial road to finish the run down the Trapline. Believe me, it's there, but go with a local if you want to find it.

TRAPLINE♦

The longest of the tree runs at Moonlight Basin goes from the mid- section of Lookout Ridge, where it starts with Ulery's Trace and Double Jack, all the way down to the base of the Six-Shooter lift. Stay right of Double Jack at the start, then hang left off Ulery's for a long delight in the trees.

Fur trappers were the original Caucasian explorers of the Montana Territory, looking primarily for beaver. This trade died out in the mid 1800s, to be replaced by mining and ranching, but the activity continues on a small scale, even around Big Sky. The trapline is a route along which a series of animal traps are set. Often many miles long, the trapper, like this run, is out in the woods awhile.

TREMBLER ■

Named before the run was cut, this is the easiest of the blue runs off the Lone Tree lift. In the valley between Lookout Ridge and the Horseshoe, it receives several of the glade black diamonds off these two other blues. It has one rather flat area midway down that requires that you maintain speed to avoid a bit of poling. Trembler means a small earthquake, or to cause one to tremble in fear; neither fits this wide gentle run. Tremble not! Just enjoy this pretty, gentle descent.

TRIDENT ♦♦

Named for the three narrow gullies that come off the rock band below the North Summit and lead into a single chute that looks like a trident. Truly extreme, this can only be skied after a climb up from Deepwater Bowl, and is not a recommended descent.

A trident, from the Latin meaning three teeth, is a three pronged fish spear that was traditionally the weapon of Poseidon/Neptune. Although next to Orbit, this is not casual gum chewing country.

TWIN TUNNELS ●

An easy route from Blue Moon to the base of the Pony Express lift, this leaves right off the middle of Blue Moon just below the Beacon Park and passes under two roads, through tunnels, to connect with Diamond Hitch.

ULERY'S TRACE ♦

Starting along with Trapline off Lookout Ridge, this keeps more right and parallels Moonshine and Ice House which it blends into before exiting into Meriwether. This is the tree route down this face, and allows for escape into the open Ice House if the woods gets too tight or intimidating.

Jake Ulery, a civil war deserter, lived and prospected the area of Moonlight Basin in the late 1880s. He created the lakes in an attempt to divert the water from the Beehive Basin into the agricultural area of the Madison Valley. His plan was halted by the Gallatin County water commissioner, but his lakes remain as a beautiful part of Moonlight Basin.

A trace means a way or route, and chiefly represents a path beaten down by the passage of humans or animals. It is in more common usage in the American southeast.

53. *Pioneers Crossing the Plains of Nebraska, C.C.A. Christensen, BYU Museum of Art, public domain*

WAGON TRAIN ●

Not named for the long running TV western potboiler, this truly western name derives from the groups of covered wagons that carried settlers and gold seekers west. Banding together for safety, these "trains" became moving miniature temporary towns. The Montana author, A. B. Guthrie, Jr. won a Pulitzer Prize in 1949 for his novel *The Way West* about this phenomenon. It is well worth the read, as is the prequel, *The Big Sky*, from which we get our area name.

Gather your friends and their wagons together and follow one another down this lazy trail that leaves mid Cinnabar halfway down on the left, and proceeds to the base of the Derringer lift.

WHISKEY ♦

The first glade run going left off Lookout Ridge drops down into the flats of Trembler. If you want to ski a black diamond glade or tree run, Whiskey should be your first choice, as it is the easiest.

It's not clear if Whiskey is a better ski run than Moonshine, but it is a slightly higher class liquor. Whiskey was the drink of choice in the Old West, probably because it was cheap and easy to make as it was distilled from fermented grain mash.

WHITE BARK ♦

Between Jackrabbit and Whiskey, this run takes the short, steep side hill from Horseshoe Bowl into Trembler. *Pinus albicaulis*, the Whitebark Pine, one of the oldest of living species, inhabits this rocky, alpine area. Most of the trees that you see high on Lone Mountain are Whitebark, or its close cousin the Limber pine. The seeds provide the primary food for Grizzly bears in the Fall. The dead trees that you see are the result of an infestation of white pine blister rust and the mountain pine beetle that killed many trees in the early 1970s. It returned, beginning in 2005, to feast and kill again.

WHITETAIL ♦ ♦

Between Three Forks and Class 4, is this steep, extreme chute. In the Headwaters, the water theme is broken with this name which was the I in ELVIS in the Nashville Bowl days. Patroller Alex Hassman said that if you look up to this run in a low snow year it looks like the back or tail end of a white tailed deer. Please do not ask how this image came to him.

White tailed deer,   Tom Kelly

The white-tailed deer, *Odocoileus virginianus*, or simply the whitetail is common in Montana. Found in river bottoms and prairie areas, its cousin the mule deer is the one that you will see in summer around Moonlight Basin.

WHITEWATER AREA ♦ ♦

Following the water theme of the Headwaters bowl - we now find whitewater. For those of you that are unfamiliar with river canoeing or kayaking, even though this is a ski resort, the white does not refer to snow on the water. Instead it refers to rapids, and whitewater on a river gives bumps like moguls on the mountain - and is fast and steep.

Approached after a climb, and very rocky, the extreme runs of Class 4, 5, and 6 in the Whitewater area are here and referenced previously.

YAAK ●

This green run under the Derringer lift from Stage Fright to Cinnabar was named for an area in NW Montana. The Yaak River there that drains into the Kootenai River has been made famous by author Rick Bass with his writings such as *The Book of Yaak*, and *Winter: Notes from Montana*.

It was not named for the Himalayan bovine animal, nor the sound of out of control skiers.

ZERO GRAVITY TERRAIN PARK

Found off the end of Runaway or from Park Avenue, this is one of the best terrain parks around. Full of fun features and entertainingly visible from the lift, it is loved by young skiers and boarders.

Older skiers and riders with more brittle bones are advised to keep their feet on the ground and stick to cheering the young ones.

Lone Mountain Ranch, Dining Lodge in snow   *courtesy LMR*

LONE MOUNTAIN RANCH

Tucked in the woods just above Big Sky's Meadow Village is Lone Mountain Ranch. A year around guest ranch experience, it is also a premier cross country ski resort. Rated the #1 Nordic ski center in North America by a Cross Country Skier Magazine reader's poll, it boasts over 90 km of groomed trails, lovely cabins, and a superb restaurant.

Unlike Big Sky and Moonlight Basin which were carved de novo out of Forest Service and Plum Creek Timber lands, Lone Mountain Ranch has a long history. First homesteaded in 1915 by Clarence Lytle, it was purchased in 1926 by Chicago paper mill tycoon Fred Butler and named the B Bar K. Some of the cabins that he had built are still in use, and pieces of Mrs. Butler's Indian artifact collection still hang on the dining room's walls. Sold in 1946, and changing hands several times, the Ranch became a logging camp, a boy's ranch, a working cattle ranch, and eventually a guest ranch. It's historical significance was honored with the placement in 2006 on the National Register of Historic Places.

Renamed Lone Mountain Guest Ranch when Jack and Elaine Hume bought it in 1955, it was eventually sold to Chet Huntley's Big Sky project in 1969. Although informal cross country ski races were held when it was owned by Big Sky, the Ranch properties were used primarily to house VIP guests. When Boyne purchased Big Sky in 1976 they did not opt to include the LMR portion. This made it available, and in 1977 it was purchased by Bob and Vivian Schaap.

Originally from Wyoming, the Schaaps had run a cross country operation in West Yellowstone for five years. With the availability of the old B Bar K, they saw the opportunity to create a first class guest ranch and the first Nordic ski resort in Montana. Unwilling to be just a "dude ranch" or offer a few groomed tracks, the Schaaps developed a diverse experience with children's and naturalist programs, first class instruction, and a stimulating culinary experience. An understanding with the Big Sky Owner's Association (BSOA) has led to extensive trail grooming on the golf course, and conservation easements now preserve the upper trails. Bob and Viv retired and sold the Ranch in 2007, but their tradition of excellence continues.

Whether you are a skater or classic skier, there are always freshly groomed trails to enjoy. The tracks on the golf course in the Meadow Village are flat and easy, whereas those on the upper mountain will have climbing and downhill schusses. If you are having trouble with the technique, or are just new to XC, the ski school instructors are excellent and are ready to help. The trail maps, available at the Nordic Ski Shop in the A-frame, or on the website at http://www.lonemountainranch. com/winter/trailmap/ , are clear and all the trails are well signed with names and numbered posts corresponding to the map. The maps also indicate hills, distances, and elevation to help prevent the grumbles.

The following list represents all of the official cross country tracks and snowshoe trails. Distances are in kilometers (1.6 to the mile) from the A-frame unless otherwise indicated. The trails are designated as beginner ●, intermediate ■, or advanced ◆. Beginner trails are relative flat and suitable for all ages and levels. The intermediate runs require some uphill technique and the ability to control your speed with a snowplow on the downhill sections. Those marked advanced are significantly steeper and will have some herringbone sections on the ascent with speedy sections on the return. This is aerobic exercise at altitude, so carry water for hydration, and check the distances so that you don't exceed your energy limits.

Whether you are skiing on the open views of the Meadow trails, in the deep climax forest along the North Fork creek, or getting a workout on the upper trails; there is a world of skiing to enjoy. And when you are done, a hearty lunch at the Dining Lodge, or libations at the bar, are there for you.

Schi Heil!

Further information on the Ranch and activities is available at www. lmranch.com. The daily grooming and conditions can befound by calling the outdoor shop at 406-995-4734.

ANDESITE ■ 8.5 km

From the A-frame, go up the 100 yards to post #1 and turn left to follow the North Fork downhill and through the tunnel under the highway. Once you cross the bridge over the Middle Fork and hike up to #33 you can loop either direction. Counterclockwise is an easier climb as you follow the Middle Fork along the willow bottoms (moose habitat), through the Aspen Groves subdivision, and over above the Hidden Village condominiums. The downhill section to the Tree Farm is a steady, winding trail needing your snowplow for turning and speed control. In an ideal world the ski trails would have preceded the development as part of the infrastructure, but this one has had to follow the lot lines in Aspen Groves. Still, it is good that they were permitted as the homes are interesting, and the trail a lovely, hilly loop. Although much altered from the early days, this route was once used for training by the US Olympic team.

XC Skiing fun   *Rumsey Young*

It was named for the mountain and ridge that it is on. Andesite is a volcanic, igneous rock related to basalt and granite. It tends to be found at the edge of tectonic plates and gets its name from the Andes Mountains of South America

ANTLER RIDGE ■ 2.0 km spur

This serves as a feeder trail to the Antler Ridge subdivision. It does not have any other destination or particular views.

Antlers are the usually large, complex "horns" on the heads of most deer species. Unlike horns, these are shed after the rut each year and grown again in the Spring. The antlers tend to be shed in certain areas, note Shedhorn Mountain south of Big Sky, and they tended to be found on this ridge before the development.

An interesting fact was discovered recently by researchers. In addition to obvious display and defense, and the known temperature regulation, it now appears that antlers act as large hearing aids. Moose with antlers have far more sensitive hearing than moose without, as the antler behaves like a parabolic reflector.

BEAVER SLIDE ♦ 1.8 km loop

This loop is an exciting alternative to the Middle Fork or Andesite trails. Run counterclockwise, it seems quite gentle until you find yourself at the top of a very steep drop back down to the Middle Fork. As you pass the bottom of the slide on the way up the Middle Fork trail, do not be alarmed by the large holes in the snow off the trail to your right. Your skill on the boards is better! You <u>will</u> make the turn and not go splot in the snow like those other people did.

There is a lot of beaver activity in this willowy section of the Middle Fork, so look for the dams. These animals hibernate during the cross country ski season, but can be seen busily working in the summer. In the early years of the Ranch, horses were pastured in what is now Aspen Groves. When wrangling them back to

91

the ranch, the route went down this trail and was in Bob Schaap's opinion, "slippery as Hell". So the trail's name originally came from horseback riding rather than skiing, but either way it works.

BOOMERANG ◆ 13 km

This rolling trail has great views and serves as an out and back feeder to the upper trails. As a run in itself it is thirteen km up to #21 and back. However, it is great as a return after reaching Siberia, Mongolia or Summit from the North Fork/Mountain View direction as good, consistent speed can be maintained on the downhill.

Named by the cross country ski staff, it is shaped a bit like the Australian aboriginal weapon. Like a boomerang, if done properly, it goes out and comes back.

BULLWINKLE'S (ss)

This short snowshoe loop goes out into the woods around the stables. The local moose use this area as a calving ground, and the babies are frequently seen in the Spring.

For those of you that remember the TV cartoon "Rocky and Bullwinkle," you will know where the name comes from. Neither moose nor squirrels at Lone Mountain Ranch have been seen to talk, however.

CARLIN'S CRUISE ■ 4.5 km

This extension to the Ranch Loop connects #4 on the North Fork with #23 on the Ranch Loop. The 1 km long, flat section goes through some old growth Douglas Firs. It can be skied in either direction.

Phil and Dave Carlin from Ohio were frequent visitors to the ranch and stepped in, along with the Browns and Dr Eggers when Mike Ankeny wanted out of the original partnership with the Schaaps. They were also responsible for the location and building of the Ridgetop Lodge. Since this trail cruises right by the lodge, it seemed appropriate to name it for them.

CREEKSIDE (ss)

Obvious for the location, this snowshoe trail goes downstream from the A-frame along the North Fork stream. The North Fork of the Gallatin River is a particularly healthy creek with a good population of aquatic insects that support a large and varied collection of Cutthroat, Rainbow, and Brook trout. Clear and fast, this stream remains open except in the coldest of weather. Snow pillows on the rocks as it bubbles through the huge spruce/fir forest, make for a peaceful and tranquil scene for you to enjoy and absorb.

DUTCH'S DETOUR ■ 9 km

A 1 km section can be a run in itself from #7 on the North Fork trail, or it can be used as a return off Boomerang. Either way, it makes a lovely meander in and out of some open meadows.

If you wonder why there is a trail that so closely parallels the Ridge Run, you need more horse sense. Dutch was the Schaap's daughter's horse. It was one of the old originals that came with the ranch and had its own mind and way back to the barn. This run follows that horse's trail. In fact, several of the original runs were laid out following horse trails. The old horses knew the woods and some of these trails would not have been found without the horses leading the way.

FANNY'S FLING ♦ 0.8 km segment

This steep trail is best skied downhill from #22.5 on Joy's Loop to #24.5 on the Ranch Loop. A short 1.5 km return counterclockwise on the Ranch Loop will get you back to fling down it again.

Fan Brown was the matriarch of a Chicago area family that started coming to the ranch from the very early days. They loved LMR and the whole family would gather there for vacations. When Mike Ankeny wanted out of the original partnership, she was one the people, along with Carlins and Eggers, who bought a share that prevented subdivision, and helped preserve the ranch as we know it. The run was named in honor of this special lady at her 70th birthday party.

FAR EAST ● 2 km segment

This 2 km extension of the Silverbow Loop in the Meadow starts at #27 and goes through the Community Park. Although this is listed as 13 km from the Ranch, most people use it directly by parking their car at the park on Little Coyote road. Named because it is the farthest east of any trail at LMR, it is designated as a "dog run". Since dogs are banned from the other LMR trails because their tracks degrade the grooming, it seemed appropriate to give them a special place. In the summer as well, at any time of the day, people and their dogs can be found along this trail getting exercise and fresh air.

JOY'S LOOP ● 0.5 km loop

Part of the Ranch Loop complex, this little loop rides the ridge above the Ranch for some easy rolling tracks and beautiful views. It was named for Joy Wilson, an early employee of the Ranch. Joy loved to ski, but not too far... Since she used this loop so much on her lunch break, it was named for her.

LITTLE BAVARIA/ WALKIN' JIM'S WAY ■ 10 km

The premier forested run at Lone Mountain Ranch follows the North Fork of the West Fork of the Gallatin River. Take the North Fork counterclockwise from #3 to its junction with Little Bavaria at #5. From here is is shaped like the eye of a needle with the loop section done clockwise. There are great views of Yellow Mountain with its snowfields

Skiers on Joy's Loop   courtesy LMR

and pinnacles along the way, and a nice resting bench with open views at the top of the loop.

One special place on this run is "ice box alley" that is found shortly after the entrance to the top 3.7 km loop. The track goes briefly downhill into a natural depression that, winter and summer, is several degrees cooler than the surrounding forest.

Another special attraction to this run is the fact that the area was missed by early loggers. As a result you can see a great example of an old growth climax forest. After a fire, the forest returns to a meadow. The, first invading plants are the aspen and grasses followed by lodgepole pines. These provide shade for the healthy germination and growth of the final stage of Engleman spruce and subalpine fir which you see here. These climax forest trees will live for many hundreds of years until they are struck down by disease, fire, or man.

Big Sky Snow Striders on Little Bavaria
Rumsey Young

Named because it is a special forested out of the way place, the trees give a feeling of the south German alpine country.

MEADOW VILLAGE TRAILS ●

The Big Sky Arnold Palmer designed golf course hosts a whole series of groomed beginner trails. Among these are Yellowstone, Silver Bow, and Far East - all described separately. From the Ranch it is just a few kilometers via the Ranch Loop clockwise to #24 and down Crail Creek to the Meadow. Alternatively, the Ranch Loop counter clockwise to #34 under the highway, through the Tree Farm to #31, and a short walk of a block or two on Little Coyote Road, will also get you to the Meadow Trails.

It is also possible to park at the Community Park, the Meadow Village Center, the Chapel, or at the golf clubhouse (closed in winter) at the end of Black Otter Road. Trails are near all of these sites, but, please be sure to buy a trail pass at the Ranch's Nordic Ski Shop before starting.

You may notice a series of "daisy-chain" alternative loops to all of the runs on the golf course. Of course these were made for more enjoyable variations as you ski around the meadow. They are also a cooperative effort between the golf course and the Ranch groomers to try to control the voles. These little short-tailed relatives of the mouse are very prevalent in Big Sky. They are active all Winter in the sub-nivean (under snow) world burrowing and chewing away at the turf, and their wandering tunnels make quite a destructive mess of the golf course. The extra loops compress the snow under the tracks and are designed to keep the little vermin in the rough and out of the fairways.

MIDDLE FORK ■ 13.5 km

Named for the Middle Fork of the West Fork of the Gallatin that flows along this trail, the run follows a road grade along the creek all the way up to the base of the Thunderwolf lift at Big Sky - 400' above the A-frame and just 600' up from the lowest point.

For an easy alternative, with no climbing, you can go back in time to the 1970s when Big Sky skiers would follow this road down to the Yellow Mule Saloon in the Meadow. Hitch a free ride on the Skyline shuttle bus to the Mountain Village. A short walk to the bottom end of Low Dog Road takes one to an entrance to the Low Dog cat track that goes to the bottom of the Thunderwolf lift. The first steep section can be walked, and from there it is a long steady downhill to the ranch or the Meadow Village trails. The Yellow Mule Saloon is long gone, but La Luna and the Lone Peak Brewery have better fare anyway.

When Big Sky was first built, the water and sewer lines were laid under this road. In the early 1970s, a skier came into the Schaap's place in West Yellowstone, and said that they had been cross country skiing around Big Sky. When asked where, the skier said , "Down the Middle Fork." "Oh," Bob said, "you mean the "poop chute!"". That name had stuck and that is how this run is now known to the locals. It makes a nice mountain bike ride in summer, and, because it is geologically much more stable, this road was preferred by the Montana Highway Department as the way to get up to the Mountain Village. The ski resort developers wanted the current highway location, as it is south facing and made snow removal less of a problem. The resort people won and the highway department has had to deal with Lone Mountain Trail slumping into the valley, while we get to enjoy a great XC ski.

MONGOLIA ■ 20 km

At 20 km and 1700 feet above the A-frame, this is one long trek. However, you won't be cold; and with a lunch packed for sustenance, and plenty of water you will be rewarded with stunning views and a ripping return down to the Ranch.

Way far away, this was named for its remote location. Genghis Khan and the horde have been reported to have been sighted up here. Not to worry, they are apparently friendly and after that long climb, your tongue will be hanging out so far that you won't care. I understand that the mare's milk and yak butter tea is exceptional.

MOUNTAIN VIEW ■ 9 km

One of the lovelier loops at the Ranch, the long trip up the North Fork is rewarded with a spectacular view of Lone Mountain towards the outer end of the loop. Done counterclockwise from post #11, the trip down is fast, and rolling as the trail descends out of the forest. It gives an exciting thrill as

View from Mountain View   *J. Strickler*

95

a reward for the work of the climb.

Unrelated to the local hardware store of the same name or the suburban San Francisco Bay area town, this is a truly Montana experience.

NATURE TRAIL (ss)

The Ranch has always prided itself on the interpretive studies of the area. A Nature Trail was naturally a necessity, and this short snowshoe trail near the Ranch base allows study at a leisurely pace. Lone Mountain Ranch has a full time naturalist staff who will lead interpretive snowshoe hikes on the Ranch, or guided ski tours into the Lee Metcalf Wilderness and the NW corner of Yellowstone Park.

Herb on North Fork, Junction to Everywhere
courtesy LMR

NORTH FORK ■ 7 km

This 7 km loop is a nice run by itself with the creek, trees, views and some swift downhill sections. It is also the connector to Little Bavaria and all of the upper trail system. As such, it gets the heaviest use of all the LMR trails.

This loop is steep at first if done in the counterclockwise direction. It is more mellow going uphill run clockwise, but leaves quite a zip on the return. It was so named because it follows the North Fork of the West Fork of the Gallatin River. We also have a trail, mentioned above, along the Middle Fork, and the South Fork can be found on the Ousel Falls trail. The forks come together in the Meadow Village to form the West Fork which enters the main Gallatin River near the Conoco station at the entrance to Big Sky. With all of the scenic and historic events in this valley, no one has explained why our river has such boring names.

RALPH'S OUTLOOK ♦ 14 km

This clearly expert trail starts from the Crail Creek connector between the Ranch Loop and the Meadow trails at post #25. This means that you can start from either the Ranch or the Meadow Village for this trip. Remote, and deep in the woods, there are six pitches on the way up that require a herringbone, and the steep return to #25 can be done in 15 minutes. ZZZZZZip!

Named for Ralph Brown, son of Fanny, Bob Schaap has said that, "his contributions to the Ranch were enormous". When Mike Ankeny wanted to sell his part of the Ranch for real estate development, the Browns were among those that stepped in to save it. Ralph's knowledge of conservation real estate created a conservation easement plan that has become a national model of what can be done in a resort community. Without his vision, there would not have been a viable cross country system and this would have dramatically changed the Ranch. Sadly, while at the Ranch and working on a project, Ralph suffered a pulmonary embolus and died. He was 43 years old.

Ralph's Outlook not only refers to the beautiful view from the bench at the top of the run, but also to his outlook or vision that was one of the redeeming ideas that preserved the Ranch.

RANCH LOOP ■ 6 km

The easiest and most popular loop out of the Ranch, it is the one that most people use for their first experience after arrival.. The Ranch Loop is groomed every night, so conditions are always best. The easy rolling ups and downs give great views of the Meadow Village and of Lone Peak.

RIDGE RUN ■ 8 km

This is an alternate route to Dutch's Detour, coming down off Mountain View or Boomerang. It provides a fast, tight downhill that leads into Schaap's Schuss,

Bob and Viv Schaap   *Courtesy LMR*

SCHAAP'S SCHUSS ♦ 0.4 km loop

This short loop at the end of Dutch's Detour and Ridge Run, or up from Sluice Box provides an exciting downhill with an easier uphill return. It is always done clockwise. The naming of this run was a bit ironic. The original route of the trail had skiers going up the steep hill. Bob hates to herringbone and this was his least favorite run at the Ranch. In his honor, the route was reversed so that Schaap's Schuss became a downhill and a more appropriate route for the scion of the Ranch. In skiing, a schuss is a straight downhill at high speed. Yiiii! Ha!

View from Siberia   *Rumsey Young*

SIBERIA ♦ 16 km

Cold and far away, the run got its name because it is so remote This was the highest and longest trail in the resort's early days, but now Summit and Mongolia go even farther. The young racers can make short work of the climb and distance on this run. Well groomed for classic, diagonal stride skiing, those of us of an older and slower bent pack a lunch and make an all day trip of Siberia. Hey! You get great views and no gulags!

SILVER BOW ● 5.5 km loop

The main trail in the Meadow complex loops around the Silver Bow condominiums. Along with Yellowstone, this is the easiest of the cross country trails and the perfect place to perfect your skating technique. Moose frequent the lower elevation of the Meadow in the Winter, and are often seen along this trail. The best places to find them are in the willows between the 2nd fairway and Spotted Elk Road, by the warm spring below the chapel, and in the woods by the bridge on the western end of this trail. Keep your distance if you see one. They may appear to be big funny looking cows, but they are fast and dangerous. More people are injured by moose than bears.

The original condominium complexes in Big Sky were all named for Montana counties. Silver Bow, whose seat is Butte, comes from Silver Bow Creek. The area gained fame as the world's largest copper producer after WW II, but the original strike and mining was for silver. Sounds pretty, but because of the mining and smelting, Silver Bow Creek is one of the country's largest Superfund sites.

"The Prospectors" Lyndon Pomeroy, 1974,
J. Strickler, courtesy City of Helena

SLUICE BOX ■ 6 km

A sluice box was used in placer mining to process more gravel than panning. A box was built with ridges on the bottom and the stream was directed through the box and gravel was shoveled in. The heavier gold would settle and be trapped on the bottom ridges, and the gravel washed away.

When this trail was first cut it had lots of quick up and downs , a "washboard" effect, rather like the ripples in a sluice box. It has since been changed, and now curves back and forth around an open meadow side hill where it provides a great introduction to the upper trails.

The trees are interesting here as the larger older ones have trunks that bend sharply uphill before rising straight to the sky. This is because of the instability of the soil on this side of the Westfork. The ground is slowly slipping down towards the river. Instead of the trunks bending uphill, in actuality, it is the roots that are moving downhill.

SUMMIT ♦ 18 km

The highest point on the Lone Mountain Ranch trail system, this is one of the more recent trails and is truly near the summit. Cresting at 8350', it is nearly 1800' above the Ranch, and 700 feet above the Big Sky Mountain Village base area. You won't get a climb like this in the Midwest.

Packer on the Upper Trails
courtesy LMR

TOWN CENTER TRAILS●

These were instituted in 2009 and are being expanded to provide access and exercise on our most recent community development area.

TREE FARM ■ ● 3.5 km

Named for all the trees the run passes, this short loop provides access to the Andesite, Middle Fork, and Meadow trails. It has a very steep section on the eastern end, so good downhill control is essential.

ULLRS (ss)

This is the snow shoe trail for the strong of heart. Leaving the Nature Trail, it crosses Mountain View several times, then parallels Siberia and goes to the "view point" at the end of Mongolia. The top here is at 8250', a 1700' elevation gain from the Ranch. Ullr is an early Norse god whose name meant "glory". He is now treated rather like a troll and worn as a good luck charm by skiers.

Ullr pin   *J. Strickler*

YELLOW MOUNTAIN (ss)

Heading up the hillside from the Nature Trail at about ski post #4, the trail loops in the forest on the southwest shoulder of this mountain. This prominent peak, elevation 9442', rises up to the east of the ranch and is the dominant rise above the Meadow Village. The west side of Yellow Mountain provides the backdrop to the North Fork stream as one ascends Little Bavaria, with the pinnacles or hoodoos prominent against the snow.

Yellow Mountain   *Rumsey Young*

There are several wide open meadows on this mountain that provide some great turns for backcountry climbers. Unfortunately, these areas have deep and unstable snow. It was the scene of the death in an avalanche in March 2007 of Ben Richards of Bozeman.

YELLOWSTONE ● 4 km loop

This run was named for the Yellowstone condominiums, which were in turn named for the Montana county, with Billings as the seat. The county comes from the river that it straddles and not the National Park. However with the Park our cozy neighbor just 20 miles south on Highway #191, it is an appropriate allusion.

One of the first trails developed, it originally circled the Yellowstone condos, but new construction years ago demanded rerouting. It now goes around the Glacier condos, and the Yellowstone ones can only seen from the southwest end of the Silver Bow loop, but the traditional name persists.

This rerouting was necessitated by easement difficulties with some private property that was developed. This and the problems engendered by the withdrawal of Mike Ankeny from the Ranch partnership show how critical easements are to this, or any resort. Fortunately, thanks to Ralph Brown, these have all been resolved. The end result for the Yellowstone loop in the Meadow has been the addition of an extra 1.5 km loop around golf holes 8 & 9 which adds a bit of variation, and an excellent practice area for skate skiing.

WALKIN' JIM'S WAY

Named Little Bavaria for the first 34 years of the Ranch, this run was renamed Walkin' Jim's Way for the 2010-11 season in memory of Jim Stoltz. Walkin' Jim was a long distance hiker, poet, songwriter, environmentalist, and a troubadour for the past 30 years at Lone Mountain Ranch. He died of cancer in September of 2010. What a fitting trail for him

Deep snow at LMR   *Rumsey Young*

BACKCOUNTRY SUGGESTIONS:

In addition to the beautifully groomed trails at the Ranch, there are many opportunities for untracked backcountry skiing adventures around here as well. Wider backcountry skis with the bigger boots and stronger bindings are available for rent at the Ranch, as well as the ski shops in the Meadow Village. The joy of breaking trail through the fresh powder is unexcelled, but be smart. Never ski alone. Let someone know where you are going. Take water, food, and a first aid kit, bear spray in the Spring, and be aware of avalanche danger.

Experienced mountaineers will use the West Fork valley to get to some real high country adventures. This is not recommended for you. You may hear of people skiing up the North Fork into Bear Basin, into the Beehive, or up on Yellow Mountain. The Madison Range, here is very vertical and quite avalanche prone. 21 year old Ben Richards was killed on the Titanic Chute of Yellow Mountain in March 2007, and MSU student, Tyler Stetson was killed in Beehive Basin in January 2008. Both were with partners and were wearing transceivers.

Better that you should enjoy one of the many safe, flatter routes, especially those in the nearby NW corner of Yellowstone Park. Guided trips to these trails are offered by the staff at Lone Mountain Ranch, but exploration with your own group also works. The following short list describes the favorites.

The stoplight at Big Sky on Highway #191 is at milepost 48, so distances to the trailhead can be calculated from there.

BACON RIND:

Located on the west side of highway #191, the trail follows the creek 2 miles to the Park Boundary. With only a 200' altitude gain, this makes an easy introduction to backcountry adventuring. The only difficulties will be the depth of the snow and the weather that day.

Go to the plowed parking area for Fawn Pass at milepost 22. The trail starts across the road on the west side and soon enters the trees, angling left up the valley. Within a half a mile you will come to the opening of a long meadow where you will need to find a snow bridge to cross the creek. Follow the edge of the trees along the north side of this meadow to its head where the wooden sign and posts mark the Park boundary. This is the end of the trip, as from here the trail gets steep and difficult to follow. Have a snack in the trees then head back. Coyotes can be seen in the big meadow, and elk hide out in the nearby trees.

BIGHORN:

Starting at the signed parking area at milepost 20.5, this long, rather flat trail follows the Gallatin River to its source. Gaining only 500' over 4.5 miles gives great views of the Gallatin Range and 10,323 Bannock Peak at its head. Wide and flat, there is no special destination so you can go as far as your interest and energy permit. In the Spring after the first thaw and refreeze, the surface can get quite firm. This makes it an especially good treat for skating.

Another favorite route in here is around the hill just to the south of the valley. It is best done with a guide who is familiar with it, as there is no designated trail. A mile and a half or so up the Bighorn track finds a small creek entering from the south. Hike along the creek then up to the ridge to your right. The hilltop has a small telemark area for play before the trail wanders down through the woods and back to the car.

Finally, the Bighorn/Fawn loop should be mentioned. At 10.5 miles, it can be very long with deep snow. However in good conditions it is quite the adventure. Go up Bighorn to the cutoff to the Fawn Pass trail at 4.5 miles, and just before campsite WB1. Turn left (North) up over the cutoff and back down the Fawn Pass trail to the highway, and a 1.5 mile shuttle to your car.

FAN CREEK/FAWN PASS:

The twin to Bighorn which it parallels is reached from the big parking area at milepost 22. The Fawn Pass trail also follows a wide open section that goes east 4 miles and up 400' to the cutoff to the Bighorn trail. This area was heavily burned in the big fires of 1988 and is just regenerating Great views to the Gallatin ridge to the east can be had all along the way.

A nice alternative is to go up the Fan Creek valley. There is a junction and a sign a mile and a half up the Fawn pass trail. Take the left fork that leads down to a bridge across the creek then up the wide Fan creek valley. Explore and enjoy, then return staying in the creek bottom until you get to the meadow near the highway and your car.

PORCUPINE:

Closest to Big Sky, this is also the lowest and most problematic for snow. Forest Service Road #653, Porcupine Creek, is 3 miles south of Big Sky on #191, just past the Ophir School. Turn east and follow the road 0.5 miles to the parking area. The Porcupine is a big open bowl giving lots of options. After following an old road in about 1/2 mile the trail forks. Left leads up a hill to rolling country. Right follows the creek to a bridge. Go over the bridge and follow along the tree line to the meadows or as far as your legs and desire will carry you.

RIVERSIDE:

This trail starts in the town of West Yellowstone, 48 miles south of Big Sky. From highway #191, the main street, turn left (east) at the stoplight on Madison Avenue one

Big Sky Snow Striders in the Porcupine
Rumsey Young

block to Boundary Street. Park here as the trail starts right across the street and immediately enters Yellowstone Park.

It is intermittently groomed for track skiing, but is best rated for backcountry travel. A long straight shot follows the telephone poles for a mile then reaches the west side of the Madison River. From here there are about 4 miles of trails that wander up and downstream along the river with great views and the possibility of seeing Park wildlife.

SPECIMEN CREEK:

The trailhead for this easy 4 mile 200' elevation gain round trip, is at a parking area a short distance off the east side of Highway #191 at milepost 26.5. A favorite of the locals, this Yellowstone Park trail is ungroomed, but usually has a good track due to the traffic. It follows the narrow valley of Specimen Creek through deep forest and small meadows. The east end was burned a few years ago and the black ghost trees remain. At 2 miles, the trail forks and the bridge on the right fork makes a nice snack stop. This right fork continues to Sportsman Lake and the left goes to Shelf Lake. Neither is recommended in Winter as they are steep with significant avalanche danger. Rather, eat your snack, enjoy the forest, and head back for some well deserved après ski.

ACKNOWLEDGEMENTS:

Any book is a compilation of experiences. Mine on this mountain have been greatly enriched by my group of skiing buddys who, with varying degrees of glee, have followed me down most of the runs in this book. To Les Loble, Keith Keller, Tommy Griggs, Irv Golden, Pat Miller, and Lance Krieg, may we have many more years of adventures. On the cross country trails, I have been joined by the members of the Big Sky Snow Striders, a group of locals who go out every Thursday to enjoy what you have read here. The operating rule of this group is that no matter what the temperature or conditions, the après ski fest is a requirement. In addition, there are also the many other friends and locals, too many to mention, that help make this place, not only the biggest, but also the friendliest skiing in America. My thanks to all.

While any errors in this book are entirely my own. I relied on many people for their knowledge and experience on this mountain. In some cases, where stories, or name derivations varied, I took the editorial license to choose the one that seemed most interesting.

I am particularly indebted to the three resorts on Lone Mountain and their general managers, Taylor Middleton at Big Sky, Ennion Williams at Lone Mountain Ranch, and Greg Pack at Moonlight Basin. Without their support, this book could never have happened. In addition, the staff of the resorts has been particularly helpful and free with their time and information. Ski patrol directors Randy Spence, from Moonlight Basin and Bob Dixon at Big Sky; and Big Sky patrollers Rich Piercy and Jon Ueland, were full of history as well as being knowledgeable about names of the runs and avalanche chutes that are not listed on the trail maps. PSIA ski instructors Jonathan Bowe from Big Sky and Moonlight's Barry Silverman, in addition to being friends and companions, were full of suggestions and local knowledge; as was the Director of Mountain Operations at Moonlight, John Knapton. Karen Lum, Moonlight's Public Relations manager, and Nancy Cooke, Director of Sales and Marketing at Lone Mountain Ranch were very helpful and also generous in supplying images for the book. Dax Schieffer, previously of the Marketing Division at Big Sky and now the Director of Human Resources, has been for the last seven years the author of "The Way I Ski It" section on the snow report. He was a great contributor of stories, advice and information. Particular thanks goes to Glenniss Indreland, Brand Manager in Big Sky's marketing department, who not only helped with images, but also was crucial in designing and preparing the book for publication.

My good friends, Rick and Susie Graetz wrote *Big Sky from Indian Trails to Tram*. It was a great resource and essential reading for anyone wanting to know the history of Big Sky. Also, a very sprecial thanks to Bob Schaap who graciously gave of his time to help preserve the history of the Ranch. If only I could have interviewed Chet Huntley...

A final thanks to my wife and best friend, Karen, who accompanies my many adventures. She has tolerated my obsession with skiing, done the editing, and has put up with my hogging the computer during the writing of this book.

-- Dr. Jeff Strickler

ABOUT THE AUTHOR:

Dr. Jeff Strickler started skiing at age five and the passion has continued. He raced in high school and college on the 250' hills of his home state of Minnesota, but learned big mountain skiing on family vacations in Aspen and Sun Valley. A year as an exchange student to Austria in 1960 was followed by a three month sojourn in 1969 just skiing in the Alps. After a residency in pediatrics at Stanford University, and a bit of military duty in Alaska, he established a practice in Helena, MT in 1975, and has skied Big Sky ever since.

Dr. Jeff and his wife Karen have owned several different condos in the area, but bought their Meadow Village home in 1993. They moved to Big Sky full time upon his retirement in 2005. Tall, dressed in black, and seldom slow, he can be seen on the slopes or cross country trails most every day of the season.

J. Strickler

NOTES ON MY SKI DAYS